PRAISE FOI

Walk This Way is an insightful, honest look at the challenging work of international ministry. From biblical perspectives rooted in scripture to practical, boots-on-the-ground examples, Paul McGuinness offers straightforward, focused wisdom on engaging with what God is doing in the world. I was convicted and encouraged, challenged and inspired, provoked and motivated.

Christi Baker
Founder and Director
Canopy Life Academy

This is a very insightful, honest and practical book that I highly recommend to every church member and church leader who is preparing to join or participate in global mission. Filled with real life stories, the right questions and biblical support, this book will help you better understand how to bring much glory to our God though partnership with indigenous leaders. It will lift up your foreign ministry to a next level.

Eugene Bakhmutsky
Senior Vice President
Russian Union of Evangelicals

Paul was an early adopter in the global partnership conversation and has become an expert in helping U.S. congregations partner with global communities for redemptive transformation. You will find Paul's experience, captured in the pages of this book, to be practical and helpful as you take your next step toward global partnerships.

Mark Fitch
Executive Pastor of Adult Ministries
Parker Hill Church, Scranton, PA

With humility and tact, Paul McGuinness insightfully shares how to partner with global churches and communities instead of showing up and pretending to know what needs to done. Having partnered with Paul, I can testify that he practices what he preaches. We've seen it in Haiti, specifically in Maliarette, where Paul's church has a dynamic partnership.

Paul McGuinness' *Walk This Way* is a must-read for anyone who is serious about partnering in God's global work. May this book be used for the advancement of the Kingdom!

Crizauld Francois
Country Director
410 Bridge, Haiti

In *Walk This Way*, Paul McGuinness reminds us that in any ministry we become involved with, God is already hard at work laying down roads for us to become involved in His wonders. McGuinness' writing style has a way of bringing the questions that many of our hearts are asking into a meaningful discussion regarding Global Ministry.

Dr. Bradley D. Friesen
Pastor of Global Ministries
Centre Street Church, Calgary

Walk this Way is a simple and easy to understand manuscript for partnership mission. It's not only rich with valuable information on how to engage in healthy partnerships, but also full of Paul's personal experiences that are very captivating. His shared thoughts and experiences takes the reader through captivating biblical truth of what it means to be the people of God in the global neighborhood.

Andrew Guuru
Country Director
410 Bridge, Kenya and Uganda

The ideas Paul writes about in this book are not just theory, they are realities our church has experienced. Several years ago, when Paul moved into his role of leadership over our church's missions program, he slowly but surely led us to adopt an entirely new perspective and approach to how we "do missions." Today we consider our global partners true partners and friends in ministry. We minister to each other and with each other. And the result has been phenomenal. Read this text carefully, it will cause you to rethink how you "do missions."

Bill Higley
Vice President of Academics
Summit University

Simply put, Paul McGuinness gets it. *Walk this Way is a* powerful and practical guide for forward-thinking missions leaders who want more than just the theoretical. Paul has a solid understanding of what it means to "*partner well.*" The principles and practical applications he outlines in his book are foundational to the work our organization (The 410 Bridge) does in the some of the poorest communities around the world. It is required reading for all 410 Bridge staff and we are grateful for it.

Kurt Kandler
Executive Director
410 Bridge

In our increasingly connected world, Paul McGuinness delivers a compelling, insightful perspective on how we can best help those in need. With a focus on our God-given capacity to come alongside others in their journey, *Walk This Way* offers a renewed spirit of reciprocity in our approach to global relationships.

Tata J. Mbugua, Ph.D
Professor
University of Scranton

Walk This Way gives grace-filled answers to questions on compassion and development. It offers practical ways to engage community partners into genuine self-development and meaningful, long-lasting change. This is a must-read for anyone interested in having a positive global impact on current and future generations.

Rev. James Mwangi
Pastor
Deliverance Chapel, Karogoto, Kenya

Finally . . . a book about a healthy approach to missions that is both practical and thought-provoking. Whether you are a seasoned mission's pastor or just exploring the idea of international service, this book is for you. Paul McGuinness' approach to global ministry can help anyone desiring to strategically engage in God's global work. It challenged me, and I have no doubt it will challenge you.

Billy Nolan
Director of Global Partnerships
North Point Ministries, Atlanta, GA

Walk This Way by Paul McGuinness is a quick and easy read on the indispensable components of partnership in mission. Paul's insights are born from the hard lessons of experience and a deep desire to help the church wholeheartedly serve Christ. *Walk This Way* takes the reader through profound biblical truths of what it means to be the people of God in the global neighborhood. If you or someone you know is new to partnership in the gospel, *Walk This Way* is a strong first step.

Daniel Rickett
Executive Vice President
She Is Safe

I have known Paul for 20 years as both a friend and a fellow pastor. Through Paul's leadership, our church has adopted a global outreach strategy that has produced amazing results in our partner communities, and has captured the hearts of our people. The ideas described in *Walk This Way* will open your eyes to the beauty of the global church and give you a bigger vision for what can be accomplished in partnership with our brothers and sisters in other cultures. If you are serious about making a lasting difference in this world, this book will show you how.

Mark Stuenzi
Lead Pastor
Parker Hill Church, Scranton, PA

The world has changed but global missions has stubbornly and most assuredly tried to stay the same. In *Walk This Way*, Paul McGuinness invites us to walk with him, slashing our way through the underbrush of tried and true methodologies of the past to discover new realities and more effective ways to make disciples in all the nations.

Eric Swanson
Leadership Network
Co-author of To Transform a City

Walk This Way is a fabulous primer on cultivating healthy global partnerships. I can think of no other book that marries thoughtful theological reflection with so many invaluable principles and helpful tools. No doubt it will be in high-rotation as I re-read it, recommend it, loan it, teach it, and learn from it all over again. All the while, celebrating (with it) God's glorious plan to make Himself known by calling all peoples into Gospel partnership!

Jeanette Thomas
Pastor of Extension Ministries
Christ Community Church, Kansas City, KS

Walk This Way
A New Path To Global Engagement

Dr. Paul McGuinness

181 PUBLISHING
ATLANTA, GEORGIA

DEDICATION

To the courageous men and women of God
who are making His presence visible across the globe:
people like John and Mark Volmink,
Julian and Joanna Thomas,
and Jenni Arendorf in South Africa;
Pastors Harrison, James, Charles, Stephen,
David and Robert in Kenya;
and Paul Appolon and Rose-Carnie Elysee in Haiti.

Your character, leadership and passion for Jesus
make it obvious that
"the LORD is in this place."

CONTENTS

ACKNOWLEDGMENTS

Countless people have played a part in my journey and in the writing of this book. I'm grateful for each one of them. Below are some of those who stand out.

I can't thank God enough for my family. My parents, siblings and in-laws continually provide an unbelievable amount of encouragement and support. I'm especially grateful for my wife, Aimee, and my kids, Mattie, Jackson, Andie and Ella. Your love, patience, and confidence has made the process of writing, editing, and refining this book possible. If God gave me nothing more than the five of you, I'd be a blessed and happy man.

God has given me a fantastic "second family" in my small group community. Each person has played a part in my life and in this book. Tony and Jill, Aaron and Carin, Scott and Katy, Duane and Daylin, Dave and Anna, Ada, Ryan and Chiara, Matt and April, Glen and Mary, and Tom and Sharon, friends like you are rare. There's always a place for you in my heart and around my table.

Two mentors gave me timely and life-changing advice that altered my trajectory and made this book a reality. Dr. Jim King, with his vision of a new model for global engagement, planted the seeds for everything you will read in this book. Dr. Darren Kizer, with his encouragement to further my education and sharpen my focus, gave me the push I needed to earn a doctorate and write a book.

Writing is a long, lonely process. Several friends provided invaluable encouragement and much-needed editing. I truly appreciate Steph Whitacre, Ken Knelly, Dan Rickett, Eric Swanson and Carol King.

All of the ideas for global partnerships found in *Walk This Way* would have been nothing more than theories had it not been for two leaders and the opportunities they offered me. Mark Stuenzi and the leaders and people of Parker Hill Church provided me with a platform to build a new model for global ministry. Kurt Kandler and the team at The 410 Bridge came into my life at just the right time, shared a common vision, and walked the path with me. I truly believe that together we've been able to do exponentially more than what we could have done on our own.

My deepest gratitude is to my Savior, Jesus. Thank you for calling me to follow You, for preparing the road ahead, for directing me step-by-step and for walking with me along the way. There is no doubt that You are building your church. Thank you so much for letting me join you in that great global work.

1 LET'S GO!

We act as if our place is on the sideline.
Actually God wants us in the action.

It was nearly midnight on New Year's Eve, and our short-term mission team was not prepared for what we were about to experience. Red African clay beneath our feet. A corrugated metal roof overhead. Simple, wooden plank benches lined up in rows and crammed with people. The room was packed. The energy was contagious. There was emotional and energetic singing, dancing, rejoicing and celebrating . . . for nine hours!

James Mwangi, pastor of Deliverance Church in Karogoto, Kenya, was hosting our team and leading the celebration. It had started at 9 p.m., hours before our team arrived, and continued until 6 a.m., long after our team crashed into their beds. The people of Karogoto were engaged in a dusk-til-dawn worship marathon, thanking the God of heaven and earth for all He had done in the previous year and crying out to Him with their hopes and dreams for the year to come.

An hour or two into the experience, Tim, one of the twenty team members from our church, took a seat to catch his breath, continuing to take in all that was going on around him. Lifting his head and looking to the front wall of the church, he noticed a banner hanging above the stage. The sign took a line from one of Israel's forefathers, Jacob, when he awoke from an unforgettable dream (you can find the story in Genesis 28). Jacob concluded, and the people of Karogoto echoed through their banner, *"Surely the LORD is in this place!"* What a fitting caption for this scene.

Looking back, Tim described it this way, "In the village of Karogoto, it may not seem like they have much: no running water, very little electricity, no cars, not enough jobs, no hope for education and very limited possessions. Their lives are filled with hard work and little reward. But in the midst of all that, if you look a little deeper, the LORD is with them. It's incredible!"

And it was. The God of the universe was in that simple village church, inhabiting the praises of His people, bringing hope for the coming year, offering comfort and healing to those who had faced tragedy, pouring out His joy into the hearts of His children. The banner described it perfectly. In between the corrugated metal roof and the red dirt floor, the LORD *was* in that place!

I am convinced that we could hang that banner anywhere on the planet. God's presence isn't limited to any one location. His work isn't confined to a continent or bound by a border. He's a global God, and He is at work – not just here but everywhere. He is drawing people to Himself, offering forgiveness and redemption. He is reaching out with care and compassion for all of us who have been beaten down by this world. He is defending and protecting the poor, vulnerable and oppressed. He is at work, giving glimpses of the restoration that is to come. Make no mistake. God is present, and He is active!

That's not all. Not only is He involved, but He's inviting us to get involved. Not only is He on the move, but He is urging us into motion. He's calling us to join Him in His life-changing, world-transforming work. This is no time to stay on the bench.

Missing the Action

If I have one regret about my short-lived athletic involvement, it's that I spent so much time on the bench. Every now and then the question comes up, "Did you play any sports in school?" The honest answer goes something like this, "I was on the team, but I didn't really play much!" I would suit up, but spend most of my time on the sideline. My favorite part was the pre-game warm-ups with my basketball team. That was one of the rare times that I got to wear the uniform *and* be on the court. You've never seen someone so excited about lay-up lines and shooting drills! I knew a seat on the bench was waiting for me once we got to the opening tip-off, and it didn't take long for me to come to the conclusion: *getting in the game is better than being on the bench.*

It was true then, and it's true now. It's true for me, and it's true for you. It's true in sports, and it's true in life. When it comes to the transforming work that God is initiating around the world – the proclamation of salvation, care of the poor, and advocacy for the oppressed – far too many Christ-followers are content to stay on the bench. We're removed from the action. We're not sure we really have anything to offer. We don't feel qualified to get in the game. We don't have piles of money lying around. And, quite frankly, we're just too busy with other things. There are way too many urgent demands for us to even think about, much less get involved in, what God is doing globally. We hope someone will make a difference, have an impact, and change the world. It's just not a real possibility for us. So we settle for the sideline.

Don't do it! Don't let any of those excuses become obstacles. Get in the game. There are simple, practical steps you can take to join what God is doing around the globe. This is your invitation to be part of the action that God is orchestrating, to be a player in the movement that He is leading. And I'm not the only one inviting you. God Himself has gone ahead of you and prepared the way. He is the One calling you out. He so badly wants you to get involved that He has made all the arrangements and cared for all the details. God has prepared the way; it's time to get going.

Preparing the Way

The Apostle Paul wrote a letter to the believers in first-century Ephesus that we now know as Ephesians. After explaining that salvation is not granted because of good works, he clarifies that salvation should lead to good works. Then he goes on to explain that God Himself has prepared the way so that His people can accomplish those good works. Paul says it this way:

> For it is by grace you have been saved, through faith and this is not from yourselves, it is the gift of God not by works, so that no one can boast. For we are God's handiwork, created in Christ Jesus to do good works, which God prepared in advance for us to do. (Ephesians 2:8-10)

There's a fascinating word picture in verse 10. God has *"prepared"* good works for us to do. The word that Paul used to describe the preparation process is the same word that first-century writers used when talking about the advance team that went ahead of a king.

Think about the President's Secret Service detail. Before the President goes anywhere, entire teams of people go ahead of him. They make sure all the logistics are in place. They figure out the best routes and plans and contingencies. They do all they can to ensure that the President can do what he is supposed to do. They *prepare* the way.

That process has been going on for centuries. It wasn't as high-tech and detailed in ancient times, but the idea was the same. The king's servants would determine the route for the king and his processional. They would widen the roads and level the paths. They would make sure there weren't dangerous drop-offs or high-risk situations. They would prepare the way for the king.

We get a glimpse of this in Matthew 21, when the people of first-century Israel wanted to appoint Jesus as their king. He was riding into Jerusalem on a donkey. What were the people doing? Laying their coats down on the road, leveling it out, making it smooth – *preparing the way*.

Now, take another look at what Paul says in Ephesians 2:10: "For we are God's handiwork, created in Christ Jesus to do good works, which God prepared in advance for us to do." Do you see who is preparing the way for whom? This is staggering. The servants aren't preparing the way for the King. Quite the opposite – the King is preparing the way for the servants! God Himself, the One who uniquely created us, who specifically designed us and went to great lengths to save us, is *preparing the way* for us!

Our God has gone before us and has made sure that everything is arranged so that we can do good works. He's widened the path, leveled the ground, ironed out the details and taken care of the logistics so that we can play a specific role in His story, a global story of redemption and renewal.

Apparently God doesn't want us to stay on the bench. He wouldn't have prepared the way for us if He did. God has drawn up the play and now He's calling our number. We're part of the starting lineup. He has gone before us and is now inviting us to walk down the path with Him, to get involved in what He's doing around the world. He says to us the same thing Jesus said to His first followers, "Follow Me."

Following the Leader

All four biographies of Jesus make it clear that Jesus had movement on His mind. Again and again, He calls potential followers off the sidelines and into the action. Here's how Mark captured that call:

> As Jesus walked beside the Sea of Galilee, he saw Simon and his brother Andrew casting a net into the lake, for they were fishermen. "Come, follow me," Jesus said, "and I will send you out to fish for people." At once they left their nets and followed him.
>
> When he had gone a little farther, he saw James son of Zebedee and his brother John in a boat, preparing their nets. Without delay he called them, and they left their father Zebedee in the boat with the hired men and followed him. (Mark 1:16-20)

There are similar accounts in Matthew 4:18-22, Luke 5:1-11 and John 1:35-51. In each one, the writer records Jesus issuing the same invitation of, *"Follow Me."*

Right from the start there was movement. Throughout His life on earth there was movement. In fact, Jesus talks about people *following* Him no less than 23 times. When He invited people to become His disciples, He expected them to move out of comfort and into adventure, out of the routine and into the unknown, out of safety and into danger, out of familiarity and into new relationships. Jesus expected His followers to follow.

And they did. The disciples left their nets, their boats, their booths, their businesses and their prior plans. They started following. With the exception of Judas, they never stopped. They got sidetracked a time or two. They hit some speed bumps and took some detours.

They nearly derailed during Jesus' final week on earth, but they found their way back. They followed to the end. That's when they realized that His last words were strikingly similar to His first.

In case His initial call to them had been forgotten, in case they were tempted to think that the movement should morph into a monument, Jesus makes His intentions crystal clear with His final words. Matthew's account is probably the best known:

> Then Jesus came to them and said, "All authority in heaven and on earth has been given to me. Therefore go and make disciples of all nations, baptizing them in the name of the Father and of the Son and of the Holy Spirit, and teaching them to obey everything I have commanded you. And surely I am with you always, to the very end of the age." (Matthew 28:18-20)

Mark captures a bit of a different angle:

> He said to them, "Go into all the world and preach the gospel to all creation." Then the disciples went out and preached everywhere, and the Lord worked with them and confirmed his word by the signs that accompanied it. (Mark 16:15, 20)

The movement was meant to continue. Jesus' ascension was not only His time, but also their time, to go. Essentially Jesus said, *"Once I go, off you go!"* There's no sign of stagnation, no slowing down, standing still or settling in. Jesus modeled three years of movement. He started with "Come, follow me." He ended with, "Go into all the world." It's pretty obvious that *Jesus came to begin a movement, not build a monument.*

It's no different today. Jesus continues to mobilize a global movement, and He invites us to be a part of it. Jesus' followers should actually be following, going somewhere, moving. We shouldn't all be going to the same places or all going to distant places. But we should all be going somewhere: across the hall, across the street, across the tracks, across the ocean, across the world.

Perhaps He's calling you into a new relationship, a different career path, greater involvement in your community, or connection with your brothers and sisters around the globe. I don't know where He's calling you to go, but I'm sure He's calling. He's calling you and me to join a movement. Are you moving? He's inviting us to go. Are you going?

Walking the Path

This book is designed to help you get on your way, and keep moving down a better path to global engagement. Here's how:

- We'll zoom out and catch a glimpse of the unbelievable, and perhaps unprecedented, work that God is doing around the world in our generation. The stories of transformation are staggering. We'll discover that no matter where you set your foot, you can truly say, "Surely, the LORD is in this place!"
- We'll identify the kind of work that God is doing in the world today, embracing patterns and principles that will enable us to join Him in ways that will lead to real transformation.
- We'll explore some of the common missteps we take when we begin down the path of global ministry. We're often driven by good intentions but, unfortunately, good intentions are not enough. In some cases we have done more harm than good.
- We'll discover that the healthiest way to get involved in international ministry is to come alongside the work that God is already doing – walking with Him and others rather

than walking alone. This isn't a solo sport. There's no need to walk alone or start something of our own. Rather, we'll learn how to partner with the people of God across the world, joining what God is already doing and locking arms with His global servants.

- Best of all, we'll realize that there are steps we can take right now to start moving down the path of global partnership. God really has prepared the way, and He's inviting us to join Him on it!

We weren't created and redeemed so we could stay on the bench and out of the action. We have the chance to be involved in something truly remarkable. God is on the move. He has prepared the way, and invites us to follow Him into all the world. What are you waiting for? Let's go!

START WALKING:
Notes and Next Steps

Walk This Way: Why?

- Because "Surely, the LORD is in this place!"
- Because being in the action is better than sitting on the sideline.
- Because the King has prepared the way for us.
- Because Jesus came to start a movement, not build a monument.

Next Steps

- *Radical* (Multnomah, 2010) and *Follow Me* (Tyndale, 2013), both by David Platt, touch on many of the themes in this chapter.
- Visit **www.WalkThisWay.world** for more on life-changing global engagement.

2 ON THE MOVE

We often ignore this life-changing fact:
God is on the move, not just here but everywhere.

It's amazing what you see when you simply start looking. When my kids were younger, I explained what a "punch buggy" is and how if you see one and call it out first, you get to slug one of your siblings. Car rides were never the same again! Every drive across town has turned into an adventure. Every errand is an all-out search. And, as you can probably imagine, they started seeing punch buggies everywhere! I'm not sure a single drive goes by without a sighting and a slug.

Why is that? Are there more VW Beetles on the road now than there were before I explained this fascinating (albeit aggressive) game? No. They were there all along. We just never looked for them. We had no reason to. But now that we are on the lookout, we see them all the time, everywhere.

The evidence of God's presence is no different. It's all around us; we just need to pay attention. We need to lift our heads, open our eyes and tune our ears. What if we were to start each day with a simple prayer like this: *"God, show me your presence today. Let me see the*

evidence of your involvement in my community and around the world." That
would change the way we approach each day, wouldn't it? There
would certainly be more excitement, a sense of adventure, a feeling
of anticipation. I see that sense of anticipation and eagerness in the
life of a character found in the Bible named Philip. He was looking
for signs of God's involvement, and he started seeing the signs
everywhere he went.

The New Testament book of Acts tells Philip's fascinating story.
We are introduced to him in Acts 6, when the twelve apostles
chose him and a few others to care for some widows in need. (*Side
note*: Because he was chosen by the twelve apostles, it's safe to
conclude that this isn't the same Philip who was already one of the
twelve apostles. Philip must have just been a common first-century
name.) We don't know a lot about this particular Philip, but in Acts
8, we do get to see him in action. Before we join him on a dusty
road in southern Palestine, let's briefly discuss what's going on
around him.

On the Move in Jerusalem

In Acts 1:8, just before He ascended into heaven, Jesus said to His
disciples, "You will receive power when the Holy Spirit comes on
you; and you will be my witnesses in Jerusalem, and in all Judea and
Samaria, and to the ends of the earth." Jesus made two promises in
these final words. First, Jesus promised that His followers would
receive power when the Holy Spirit came upon them. Second, He
indicated that His followers would be witnesses from Jerusalem to
the ends of the earth. The first promise was fulfilled fairly quickly.
The Holy Spirit did indeed come upon the disciples. He surged
into Jerusalem to fill and empower them (check it out in Acts 2).
Then, equipped with language learning far greater than Rosetta
Stone, the disciples were indeed able to be Jesus' witnesses. As
Jesus said they would, they began in Jerusalem. Peter stepped up

and declared the truth about Christ. Three thousand people responded, choosing to follow Jesus!

Needless to say, fulfilling this part of Jesus' promise was thrilling. The disciples loved being Jesus' witnesses in Jerusalem. That wasn't the full extent of the promise though. That was just the starting block, the launch pad. To actually fulfill Jesus' prediction, they'd need to move beyond Jerusalem. That would come next.

On the Move in Judea and Samaria

After a season of momentous growth and unprecedented favor (Acts 2-7), the church started feeling the heat. The tide of popular opinion turned, and persecution broke out against this new sect within Judaism known simply as "The Way." Stephen became the first Christian martyr; his noble death is recorded in Acts 7. Then in Acts 8:1-4, we see further fulfillment of Jesus' promise found in Acts 1:8:

> And Saul approved of their killing him [Stephen]. On that day a great persecution broke out against the church in Jerusalem, and all except the apostles were scattered throughout Judea and Samaria. Those who had been scattered preached the word wherever they went.

Did you catch that? Do you see where Jesus' followers went as they were scattered? Throughout Judea and Samaria. And do you see what they're doing? Preaching the word. Sound familiar? This is just what Jesus predicted and promised! They were filled with the Holy Spirit, and they became Jesus' witnesses, moving from Jerusalem into Judea and Samaria.

Here's where the story narrows in on Philip. Since he is not one of the apostles who stayed in Jerusalem, he must have been one of the the believers who was scattered throughout the area. Sure enough, we read that, "Philip went down to a city in Samaria and proclaimed the Messiah there… So there was great joy in that city." (Acts 8:5-8)

Samaria, like a modern-day county or district, included numerous cities, towns and villages. Philip went to one of Samaria's cities. He proclaimed the Messiah, and there was great joy in that city. In other words, they received his message. They embraced the good news. They began to trust and follow Jesus.

We aren't told to which city in Samaria Philip went. It's not really that important. We simply get to see one up-close example of one person's experience in one first-century city. But remember, Philip was one of literally thousands of Christ-followers who had been scattered throughout Judea and Samaria. It's safe to say that what happened to him in this place happened to lots of other people in lots of other places. Jesus' followers had become Jesus' witnesses, bringing hope and joy wherever they went. The good news had gone viral. It was a holy epidemic, a spiritual outbreak sweeping through first-century Israel!

No doubt this was a paradigm-shift for Philip and the rest of the early Christ-followers. They started to see something new. God was present, not just in the places the believers expected, like Jerusalem. He seemed to be present wherever they went. God was moving, not just in Jerusalem but in Samaria too!

On the Move to the Ends of the Earth

The excitement didn't stop in Samaria. It expanded to an even more obscure location. Acts 8:26 introduces us to a somewhat surprising turn in the story. After sharing the message of Jesus, seeing a great response and experiencing great joy in the Samarian city, Philip got some puzzling instructions: "Now an angel of the

Lord said to Philip, 'Go south to the road—the desert road—that goes down from Jerusalem to Gaza.'"

At that point, Philip must have felt what my kids feel when they are called to come in for dinner on a nice, summer evening. *"What? We just got out here! We can't possibly leave now. We're just getting started!"* That very well may have been what Philip was thinking. He had seen such a great response in the Samarian city. God was obviously moving there. Philip wasn't itching to leave yet, but apparently God had other plans. He wanted Philip to keep moving.

Think about Philip's trajectory. He was transferred from the metropolis of Jerusalem to the much smaller market of Samaria. But at least that shift was to another city. From there he was moved, believe it or not, to a location that was even more remote. He wasn't sent to a city this time. The Spirit didn't even direct him to a particular village. He was simply sent to a seemingly random road. His journey took him from the mega-city of Jerusalem to a smaller city in Samaria to a lonely road on the outskirts of town. I don't think this is the path that Philip was hoping to walk. These moves of downward mobility could have been discouraging, unless Philip truly believed that God was moving everywhere. God was moving in the city. God was moving in the town. And, as Philip would soon discover, God was moving on the desert road. God was moving, not just here or there but everywhere.

On the Move Everywhere

A quick look at a first-century map offers an interesting reminder of God's presence. We know that He was present and powerful in Jerusalem, where the action got started on the Day of Pentecost. When persecution broke out, the believers were scattered to Judea and Samaria. Then after seeing great joy and revival in one Samarian city, Philip was sent south to the road that led from Jerusalem to Gaza. If you plot those points on an ancient map, do you see what I see? Samaria, Judea, Gaza, and Jerusalem. North, south, east and west. No matter which direction you point the compass, you could boldly hang the banner that Pastor James hung in Karogoto: *"Surely the LORD is in this place!"*

Could this be one of the reasons why Jesus seemed so excited to ascend into Heaven and send the Holy Spirit to earth? When Jesus talked about His departure and the Spirit's arrival, He made it sound like it was a good thing. The disciples weren't so sure. They couldn't imagine anything better than having Jesus right there with them. His physical and personal presence next to them had to be as good as it could get. Jesus, however, kept trying to tell them that having the Holy Spirit would be even better. Perhaps after this scattering of believers took place, the disciples started to see why. Bound by the limitations of His humanity, Jesus was confined to one physical location at a time. He was on the shore of the Sea of Galilee. He was at the wedding in Cana. He was on the mountain, in the valley, in the boat, and on the water. He was at work in one place: either up north or down south, back east or out west.

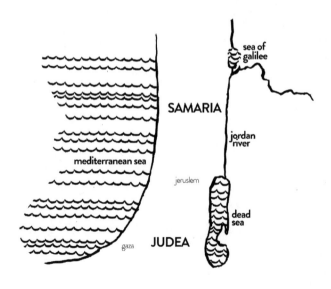

That, however, is no longer the case. Once Jesus ascended and was replaced by the Holy Spirit, geography was no longer a limitation. From that moment, the movement and presence of God could spread like the wind to the four corners of the earth! Since that shift, the gospel is not merely taking root and changing lives in one place. It is taking root and changing lives in every place! God is moving, not just here or there, but everywhere. Philip caught a glimpse of that in the first-century. If we're looking, we can catch a glimpse of it today.

On the Move Then and Now

A whirlwind trip around the world would be eye-opening. If we were on the lookout, we would see glimpses of God's involvement everywhere. If we could somehow take it all in, here's some of what we'd see, according to David Barrett and Todd Johnson's, *World Christian Trends AD 30 - AD 2200*:

- 166,000 people hearing the good news of Jesus Christ for the first time every day.
- 27 million people deciding to follow Jesus every year, 10,000 each day in China alone.
- Despite great persecution, there are more than 91 million followers of Christ in China today. In 1950, there were only 1 million.
- Many countries in Africa are poised for similar growth. The recent census of 90 million Christians on the continent is likely to explode to 1 billion by 2050.
- By 2050, the 50 million faithful in India could mushroom to 125 million.

Like any set of statistics, these numbers can't tell the whole story. The global population is also expanding, so that in many places the percentage of Christ-followers within the population is staying about the same. Nevertheless, the movement of God, especially in

Latin America, sub-Saharan Africa and parts of Asia has been undeniable in recent generations. In his article "An Upside-Down World," missiologist Christopher Wright says it this way:

> The map of global Christianity that our grandparents knew has been turned upside-down. At the start of the 20th century, only ten percent of the world's Christians lived in the continents of the south and east. Ninety percent lived in North America and Europe, along with Australia and New Zealand. But at the start of the 21st century, at least 70 percent of the world's Christians live in the non-Western world—more appropriately called the majority world.

Wright points out a mind-blowing example of this shift when he notes that there are "more people in church every Sunday in communist China than in all of Western Europe," the birthplace of modern Christianity. God is undoubtedly on the move!

Want to see for yourself? Consider the work of Global Media Outreach (GMO). A few years ago, I was able to meet Walt Wilson, the founder of GMO. He's a computer science genius, former colleague of Steve Jobs, and devoted follower of Christ. Early on, he recognized how the World Wide Web and our global connectivity could be leveraged for the gospel. According to Wilson, 91% of the people on the planet live within range of a cell tower. And, as I've seen firsthand, people all over the world have skipped landlines altogether and gotten themselves cell phones. So GMO developed more than 250 websites and mobile apps that share the good news about Jesus.

You can see all of that web traffic displayed on one of their websites at www.GreatCommission2020.com. The site tracks, in real-time, how many people around the world are interacting with one of their gospel websites or mobile apps. The counters across the bottom let you know how many have learned about Jesus, decided to trust Him, and requested follow-up! When you view the site, there is a constant flow of activity and markers popping up all over the map, acting as moment-by-moment reminders of God's global movement and perpetual evidence of His work not just here, but everywhere.

GMO estimates that 1.3 million people interact with the gospel on one of their sites every day. Roughly 100,000 make the decision to trust Jesus every day! GMO then mobilizes 9,000 online missionaries to interact with and disciple the new believers. It's a beautiful use of technology and an eye-opening reminder that God is at work, not just here but everywhere; not just in Philip's day, but ours as well!

On the Move: Not Just God But You Too

It's been said that *there are no God-forsaken places, only church-forsaken ones.* God is not absent anywhere. He has not forsaken any people or place. We will never visit a place that is not already occupied by God's Spirit. We will not beat Him to a village or a ghetto or a people group. His grace is evident. His power is on display. His Spirit is drawing people to Himself. He is actively bringing transformation across the globe. No matter where you set your foot, you can truly say, *"Surely the LORD is in this place."*

God invites you to join Him. He is not just involved; He is also inviting your involvement. He's not just on the move; He is urging you to get moving. He's calling us off the sidelines and onto the path that He has prepared for us.

As we move in that direction, let's not forget that God is already there. All too often when we begin to move, we act as if we are the ones starting the movement. We engage as though we are introducing God to a region that He has not yet visited. We walk as if we are the first ones on this path. Rather than partnering with the people of God that are already in place across the planet, we blaze our own trail and walk alone. In the next chapter, we'll explore the danger of that approach and the dead end that lies ahead if we follow that path.

START WALKING
Notes and Next Steps

Walk This Way: Why?

- Because God is on the move, not just here but everywhere.
- Because God is on the move, not just then but now.
- Because not only is God on the move, but He's urging you to get moving as well.

Next Steps

- **Global Media Outreach** is sharing Jesus online in every country of the world. Check them out at www.GlobalMediaOutreach.com and www.GreatCommission2020.com.
- In his book *The Future of the Global Church*, Patrick Johnstone, author of the phenomenal prayer guide, *Operation World*, draws on his fifty years of experience to challenge us with his bold vision of the global Christian church.
- **Operation World** is the definitive prayer guide for every nation in the world. Find out more at www.OperationWorld.org.

3 THE DANGER OF WALKING ALONE
We believe that our global engagement is helpful.
Sadly, we often do more harm than good.

On several occasions, I've had the opportunity to teach classes on global ministry. One of the conversations I like to lead students through starts with a brainstorming exercise to identify the typical pathway taken to reach the mission field. I draw a line with a cross at one end and a globe at the other. These symbols represent salvation (the cross) and full-time global ministry (the globe). The line represents the path we have created to move people toward international engagement.

Imagine someone in your church: an upperclassman in your student ministry, a young couple starting their family or an empty-nester beginning the second half of her life. That person or couple just started following Jesus and is on a path toward full-time global ministry. What does that path look like? What steps typically take place along the way?

Here are some of the items students usually add to the timeline:

- personal Bible study
- prayer
- short-term ministry trip
- formal Bible training
- gaining support from the local church
- connecting with a missions agency
- fund-raising
- learning a new language

Does anything else come to mind? Can you think of anything that should be added to the timeline? Feel free to make some edits and then take a look.

That's an impressive process! Lots of time, energy, thought and money is leveraged to prepare individuals for global ministry. There are churches and agencies that have fine-tuned this system so that seemingly nothing is forgotten or left to chance.

Unfortunately, we often do forget something – something pretty important. None of the students I've led through this exercise has ever suggested that the soon-to-be missionary develop a relationship with the people he or she intends to serve before making all these plans to go serve them. No one has looked at the timeline and inserted a stick-figure icon representing the national leaders in the receiving country. There's been no call to forge a cross-cultural relationship as part of the process. In fact, the entire plan (with the exception of a possible short-term trip) often takes place on our side of the ocean or border. Our process typically ignores the fact that God is already on the move, not just here but everywhere.

Where in this plan do we ask international leaders what God is doing in their communities? When do we listen to their assessments? At what point do we ask how, if at all, we can help? Do we let the national leaders explain where they are going and what obstacles are in their way? When do those interactions take place? Maybe in your mobilization process those things are happening. Some churches and agencies are facilitating those kinds of interactions. I am glad for this because, far too often, these components are missing.

I'm afraid to say that, for the most part, we haven't found a spot for those conversations. We haven't made room for those relationships. We've built a system that assumes that we are wanted and needed, a process that asserts our authority and lords our power over our international brothers and sisters. We don't seem to walk well with others. Far too many Westerners prefer to walk alone. We act as if we are the first ones to arrive and the only ones doing the work of God. Since we have the ability and the resources to do it on our own, we've concluded that we should just do it on our own. So we move through our process, show up in other countries and announce our arrival, assuming that the national leaders will be thrilled to see us. The trouble is, they're often not thrilled. What's even more troubling is that many of them have told us this repeatedly, but we don't seem to be listening.

They Hate When We Walk Alone

If we asked the people of God around the globe what they thought of our missions model, what do you think they would say? What would global Christians tell us about the way Americans interact internationally? We don't have to wonder what they would say. We simply have to listen.

David Livermore, author of *Serving with Eyes Wide Open*, asked twenty-three Christian leaders from twelve countries for their opinions regarding visiting Westerners, both short-term teams and long-term missionaries. Compiling the responses, he created a list that is sadly, but appropriately, titled, "Ten Things I Hate About American Missions Projects." Here are just a few:

- You act as if the American church is the true trendsetter for how we should all do church.
- You live so far above our average standard of living and you behave as if you're still in North America.
- You underestimate the effectiveness of our local church leaders.
- You too quickly get into the action without thinking through the implications on our churches long after you go home.
- We are not naïve and backward; instead, we are your brothers and sisters in Christ.

Sadly, Livermore is not the only one to receive this kind of input from global Christians. Steve Saint, son of missionary Nate Saint, wrote about the same kinds of responses from the international leaders he has come to know. One African leader said, "So many people have come to fix us. Oh Lord! Please don't bring another person to fix us." A European believer echoed that sentiment when he pointed out that foreign missionaries act like parents taking care of infants. That, in turn, prompts the local believers to "become like, 'Mama, Mama, Mama,' depending always on the Americans."

Getting that kind of feedback is no fun. It's hard to accept, but the message from global Christian leaders is clear and consistent: *Stop acting as if God is not already at work here.*

Walking Alone in Russia

Over the past couple years, I've become friends with Eugene Bakhmutsky, a prominent Russian leader. Originally from Siberia, Eugene now pastors a church and leads a historic network of evangelical pastors serving throughout Russia. He and his colleagues are no strangers to persecution and imprisonment. The price that they pay for their faith is far higher than the price that most Westerners can comprehend. In one of our early conversations, I heard first-hand what I had read in Livermore's list and Saint's book.

I asked Eugene if many North American missionaries had interacted with him and his national teammates. Of course they had. Russia has received lots of short-term and long-term missionaries, especially in the 1990's following the fall of the Iron Curtain. I asked if those interactions had been positive. I wanted to know if the U.S. teams and missionaries who had come to help had actually been helpful. Eugene wasn't eager to gripe or complain, but he was willing to share some of what he has encountered and observed over the years. He summed it up for me with three conclusions.

1. As far as he could tell, the U.S. missionaries often do not take the necessary time to understand the culture. As an example, he talked about eye contact. Americans use strong eye contact to show respect, attentiveness, and interest. Eugene explained that this is not the case in Russian culture. In his culture, eye contact is a sign of arrogance and superiority. Americans who don't take the time to learn this have consequently insulted the very people they are trying to honor.

Another example of cultural ignorance is evident whenever American missionaries handle their Bibles casually. They don't realize that in Russia, Bibles are deeply respected because they used to be so scarce. Eugene's grandfather led a church of 600 people who collectively shared one Bible! That's not necessarily the reality now, but the memory of those times is still fresh for many of the Russian believers. Enter into that setting an American youth team on their summer mission trip. As they unpack their stuff and prepare for their program, they might toss their Bibles around or set them on the floor. Every time they act so flippantly with the Word of God, their Russian hosts grimace. According to Eugene, many foreigners simply don't take the time to learn and adapt to the culture of those they are trying to serve.

2. Eugene also concluded that Western churches aren't interested in truly partnering with Russian churches. Rather than recognizing, embracing, and supporting the deep spiritual history in Russia, American missionaries forge their own paths and start their own ministries, completely independent of the indigenous Russian churches and movements. Eugene laughed as he pointed out the irony that Christianity has been alive in Russia much longer than the United States has existed as a country! Russian believers are building on literally centuries of church history, yet American Christians have the audacity to show up and take charge. For the most part, the U.S. missionaries don't want to join what is already underway; they want to start their own movement. Eugene went on to point out that, as far as he could tell, about 90% of foreign-initiated projects decline and die soon after the Americans leave. He couldn't help but conclude that the majority of U.S. churches and mission organizations just aren't interested in partnering with their Russian counterparts.

3. Finally, it has become obvious to Eugene that North American missionaries are in it for the short-term, not the long-term. They are excited to get to work; to start something and manufacture

28

some momentum. Unfortunately, there isn't much thought given to the long-term impact.

It seems like Americans don't have time for that. They feel too much urgency, so they spring into immediate action. Quick results are expected, so they get to work and get something done. Then, in many cases, they leave. Some individual missionaries may stick it out, serving for decades or even a generation. But the overall approach has been shortsighted. Very little has been developed that has outlasted the foreigners' presence and funding. The western missions model, according to Eugene, was not built with long-term development in mind.

Thankfully, Eugene could think of a few exceptions – churches and individuals, specifically the folks at the Slavic Gospel Association, who have become great friends of the Russian church. Some of those alliances have led to partnership and outreach not just in Russia, but into other countries as well. Sadly, these are the exception, not the norm.

My conversation with Eugene confirmed what I had feared. Many Western believers don't join what God is already doing. We don't often walk with others down the path. We are eager to get moving, but are either unwilling or unable to acknowledge that God is already moving. We don't need to start our own work, but for whatever reason, we often do anyway. Tragically, it seems like we often prefer to walk alone.

We're Not Trying to Walk Alone (It Just Comes So Naturally)

Foreign visitors (career missionaries, short-term ministry teams, and even tourists) bring a lot of baggage with us. We're aware of the luggage on our back, but are unaware of the chip on our shoulder. Whether we realize it or not, Americans bring a good deal of arrogance when we travel abroad. It may not be intentional, but to our hosts it is unmistakable.

In his excellent book, *Cross-Cultural Servanthood*, Duane Elmer gently but firmly points out how much pride we are packing when we arrive to serve in another culture. He says,

> Many missionaries may be like me: well intentioned, dedicated and wanting to serve, but also naïve and in some denial about what it means to serve in another culture. . . Many missionaries may be like me in another way: I am often guilty of a superior attitude. Submerged deep within me, it is evasive and hard to identify. I quickly rationalize and deny its presence. Usually superiority appears in disguises that pretend to be virtues – virtues such as
>
> - I need to correct their error (meaning I have superior knowledge, a corner on truth).
> - My education has equipped me to know what is best for you (so let me do most of the talking while you do most of the listening and changing).
> - I am here to help you (so do as I say).
> - I can be your spiritual mentor (so I am your role model).
> - Let me disciple you, equip you, train you (often perceived as "let me make you into a clone of myself").
>
> These and other so-called virtues corrupt our attempts to serve others. Superiority cloaked in the desire to serve is still superiority. It's not our words that count but the perceptions of the local people who watch our lives and sense our attitudes."

Elmer is right. Whether we mean to or not, we often embody a posture of superiority rather than a Christ-like posture of humility. We truly want to help, but we arrogantly and impulsively blaze a truly unhelpful trail.

There has to be a better way. We've done enough damage. We've destroyed enough dignity. We've started enough of our own well-intentioned but, in reality, unhelpful projects. It's time to act as if God is already on the move. It's time to acknowledge that our brothers and sisters around the world are already moving down the path. Rather than starting our own stuff, let's join the work God is already doing. Rather than setting out and walking the path alone, let's walk arm-in-arm in partnership with God's people around the globe. In the following chapter, we'll explore what that approach looks like.

START WALKING
Notes and Next Steps

Walk This Way: Why?

- Because walking alone is dangerous. It ignores and undermines the work that God is already doing.
- Because our brothers and sisters around the world are inviting us to walk with them.

Next Steps

- David Livermore's developments with **Cultural Intelligence** are extremely helpful. Discover more at www.DavidLivermore.com
- Ernesto Sirolli's TED talk, **"Shut Up and Listen"** is a humorous and insightful call to stop walking alone and start listening to national leaders and local entrepreneurs.

4 STOP STARTING AND START JOINING

*We tend to think we need to start a new movement.
Instead we should join the movement that God has already started.*

Last summer my wife, Aimee, decided it was time to repaint our
kids' bedrooms. She went with pink for the girls' room and
camouflage for our son's room. After we chose colors, it didn't
take long for the project to get underway. Drop cloths, paint cans,
rollers and brushes were brought out in full force. The rooms
began to transform.

As you imagine that scene, let's play out a hypothetical scenario.
Assume for a minute that I am both allowed and eager to help with
the painting project (did I mention this is a hypothetical situation?).
Driven by a deep desire to assist with the room transformation, I
swing by the hardware store one day after work. I tell a couple of
the employees what I'm setting out to do, and they get really
excited about it. They want to help by discounting some cans of
paint and donating some gently-used supplies. I know these
supplies and paint colors are probably not what Aimee would have
picked, but I'm sure she'll be fine with my decision to move
forward anyway. I grab some paint, tape, and brushes, and head
home excited to get started. Since I'm more into camo than pink, I
decide to focus my energy on my son Jackson's room. I pop open

the cans of green and brown paint and start slapping color on the walls. I'm energetic, excited, and driven. I think to myself, *"Just wait until Aimee sees what I've done and how helpful I've been!"* Unfortunately, I quickly realize I don't have time to finish the whole job. It's taking a lot longer than I thought it would and the work is very different than what I expected. No worries, though. I'll turn the project over to her when I've done as much as I want to do. I'm confident that I'm making a difference and pretty proud of myself for the service I'm able to provide. Just wait until I tell the guys at the hardware store! They'll be so glad they were able to support this project.

In many ways, our global interactions have looked a lot like my attempt to help with the bedroom paint project. Driven by a desire to help, the American church has assessed the situation, decided on a solution, gathered the people and resources, boarded the planes, boats or buses, and gotten to work. You don't have to look too hard to see the paint that we've slapped on walls and the marks that we've left on communities all around the world. In some cases, our efforts were appreciated and may have even been helpful. In many cases, however, our service, though it was well intentioned, was not helpful. On the contrary, many global projects have demonstrated arrogant assumptions and harmed both the people of God and the work God was using those people to accomplish in their communities. We must find a better way to approach global engagement.

Start Joining: An Ancient Example

Let's return to a story we started a few chapters ago, the story of Philip in Acts 8. When we left Philip, he was on a desert road going south to Gaza. He had been in Jerusalem and was part of an unprecedented revival. Afterward, he followed God's lead to a city in Samaria and played a part in the transformation there. Finally, he was sent to a desert road down south. No matter where he went,

34

he knew he was not alone. Whether he was in Jerusalem or the city in Samaria or on the desert road down south, he could say with certainty, *"Surely, the LORD is in this place."* He knew that God was on the move, not just here or there but everywhere. Armed with that conviction, he responded accordingly.

"So, he started out (Acts 8:27)." He followed God's lead. He obeyed the Spirit's prompting. It didn't matter where, He knew God was there. So, he started out. Let's pick up the story at that point:

> On his way he met an Ethiopian eunuch, an important official in charge of all the treasury of the Kandake (which means "queen of the Ethiopians"). This man had gone to Jerusalem to worship, and on his way home was sitting in his chariot reading the Book of Isaiah the prophet.
>
> The Spirit told Philip, "Go to that chariot and stay near it."
>
> Then Philip ran up to the chariot and heard the man reading Isaiah the prophet.
>
> "Do you understand what you are reading?" Philip asked.
>
> "How can I," he said, "unless someone explains it to me?"
>
> So he invited Philip to come up and sit with him . . . Then Philip began with that very passage of Scripture and told him the good news about Jesus. (Acts 8:27-31, 35)

What Philip did in this encounter is remarkable. Philip had seen God at work in Jerusalem and Samaria. He was confident that God was moving on that road and even in that chariot. There was never a moment when Philip felt that he was in charge. Not for a minute did he think that he had to manufacture something or force something to happen. He was well aware that God was leading this effort. So he probably didn't even give much thought to what he did next. It really was the only reasonable thing to do. Yet we seem to miss it all too often. If we could somehow reclaim this practice, it would make a world of difference. Here it is: *Philip joined what God was doing.*

Believing God was already at work, Philip followed where God was leading and joined what God was doing. He didn't start something; he joined something. He didn't set out to plant something new or launch something novel. He didn't make it about him and the work that he wanted to begin. He didn't assume he was opening a new field or pioneering a groundbreaking initiative. When he got to the chariot, Philip didn't interrupt, announce his presence, point out the Ethiopian's need and launch into his spiel. Philip took a different approach. He watched. He listened. He asked a question. He started a conversation, rather than a confrontation. Whether consciously or subconsciously, Philip acknowledged that God was already moving, speaking, and working. Philip simply put himself in a place where he could join what God was already doing.

Of course he did! That's clearly the best approach to take. How have we missed this? Where did we get the idea that we have to make something happen – open the field, plant the church, launch the Bible college, start the movement, pioneer the work? It sure seems like somewhere along the way, we forgot that God was leading, and we should be focused on joining. All too often, especially in our international ministry, we flip that over. We lead and ask God to join. We decide where to go and what is needed. We start preaching and teaching and building and fixing, fully intending to one day "turn things over to the nationals." We are eager and excited and ready to go. So we get moving and pray that God will help and bless and expand what we're doing. Sadly, we often fail to notice that God is already at work, inviting us to join Him.

Start Joining: A Modern Example

Several years ago, I was in Cape Town, South Africa. I had the chance to interact with Julian and Joanna Thomas, members of a congregation with which my church was building a relationship. The Thomases are responsible for launching a world-renowned initiative in Pollsmoor Maximum Security Prison (now known as Pollsmoor Remand Detention Centre). Terribly over-crowded, ruled by gangs and violence, this prison was once a very dark and dangerous place. Nevertheless, that didn't keep Julian and Joanna away. Driven by a desire to bring hope and transformation, they organized and continue to participate in several opportunities for Christ-followers to interact with the inmates at Pollsmoor. Once a month, they join a prayer walk that mobilizes hundreds of people from numerous churches to walk and pray through the corridors of the prison. Every other week, they host a Sunday morning worship service for the men and women there. Throughout the week, they offer classes and seminars designed to build character, trust, and life-skills. It didn't take long for them to have a significant impact. The year before they began their work, there were 297 violent incidents reported within the prison. One year later, after prayer walks, church services, and leadership seminars, there were only two such incidents reported!

The transformation at Pollsmoor was so remarkable that it drew the attention of criminal justice systems around the world. Several prisons, including one in Philadelphia, not far from where I live, invited Joanna to come and share some of her methods with them. The British Broadcasting Corporation produced two award-winning documentaries chronicling the unprecedented renewal at Pollsmoor. It really is astounding.

A few years before my visit, best-selling author, Philip Yancey spent some time with the Thomases. He included some of their story in a couple of his books. Here is a conversation with Joanna that Yancey shared in *What Good Is God?*

> These guys are monsters, rapists, murderers. And from what I see you were simply holding Bible studies, playing trust games and having prayer meetings. What really happened to transform Pollsmoor prison?

> Joanna looked up and said, almost without thinking, "Well, of course Philip, God was already present in the prison. I just had to make Him visible."

Joanna's perspective is staggering, but it rings true. She knew that she was not bringing God to Pollsmoor Prison. She and Julian were convinced that God was already present there. They weren't starting God's work. He was already at work. They were just joining what He was already doing and *making Him visible*.

God is present in the cellblock and on your block. He's at work in war-torn Uganda and in the cubicle-farm in your office. He's active in Cambodia and on your college campus. You can find evidence of His presence in Haiti and in your own home. He is present not just here and there, but everywhere. Like Philip did on the desert road, like Joanna did at Pollsmoor, you and I simply need to make Him visible. We don't need to start a new work; instead we need to join the work God is already doing.

Start Joining: The Parable Revisited

Let's return for a moment to my son's camouflage room. What if, instead of taking the initiative and making the decisions to gather supplies and begin the work, I had taken a different approach? What if, rather than starting something on my own, I joined what was already underway? If that were my focus, several of my actions would shift. For starters, I would lean into the *relationship* that I have with the one who is already at work. That person, my wife, would be more important than the project. Relationship would trump results. But the relationship wouldn't replace the results; it would simply redirect me toward better results! A simple shift in my approach (from starting to joining) would have a significant impact. Let's imagine how that scene could have unfolded.

If I were serious about joining rather than starting, then I would show genuine interest in my wife and her vision for the project. I would ask lots of questions to figure out the scope and plan. I'd affirm what she was doing and applaud how far she'd gotten already. Then, if it seemed necessary, I'd offer to help and be willing to do whatever *she* thought would be most helpful. I'd wait, listen, learn, and follow her lead. Those conversations, those relational interactions, would be the key difference between this approach and the previous one. The relationship is the turning point. That personal connection reminds me that I'm joining something that is already underway, not starting something from scratch. The focus on relationship changes everything.

Consider this: It is possible that in the course of my interaction with Aimee, it became obvious that what she really needed me to do was swing by the hardware store, pick up a can of green paint and a can of brown paint, come home and start slapping it on the walls. It's possible that the approach I wanted to take is the very approach that would be most helpful. It's possible that I would have "guessed right." It's certainly not probable though. It's much more likely that she would appreciate some help with sanding or taping. She may ask me to do a second coat in the girls' pink room while she works on Jackson's room. She may not want my help with painting at all. (This is the most likely scenario!) Because she's been working on the painting project all day, she may want me to run out and grab something for dinner. Now that would actually be really helpful. But unless I'm willing to slow down and have a conversation, I'll never know how to be most helpful. I'll never be able to actually join what she is doing unless I first lean into the relationship that I have with her.

This is where many well-meaning westerners find themselves: eager to do something but failing to do the right thing. We are well intentioned but not well informed. We lean toward results rather than relationships. We start our own stuff instead of joining God's stuff.

There is a better way, a better path to walk down. It's the path of partnership – coming alongside the people of God around the world and journeying with them into the transformation that God is orchestrating. That's an exciting journey. Let's explore it together in the following chapters.

START WALKING
Notes and Next Steps

Walk This Way: What?

- Go where God is leading.
- Join what God is doing.

Next Steps

Fikkert and Corbett's best-selling, *When Helping Hurts* was a ground-breaking and much-needed manual for caring for the poor. Even several years after its release, *Christianity Today* called it the "poverty fighter's Bible."

5 LEARNING TO WALK TOGETHER

We've convinced ourselves we've got all we need.
The truth is, we are just one part of a global body.

Walking alone is dangerous and unnecessary. It's time to forge a
new path, one that we'll walk together. The traditional model of
global engagement must give way to a new approach that enables
and encourages us to build healthy partnerships with God's people
around the world. The model below leads us down the wrong path:

You may not find this image on the wall of a church or missions
agency, but it's a pretty good picture of our typical approach to
global engagement – the West to the Rest. What we erroneously
communicate to the rest of the world is that we've got it figured

out and will be right over to show you how to do it. "It" can be anything. In the model above, it's church. We've figured out the buildings, the programs, the leadership style, the organization, the systems, and the way to train men or connect with women or mentor children. We have the most relevant approach to Scripture and preaching, the best songs to sing and instruments to use, the correct Bible translation, and the list goes on. As soon as we can, we'll fly over to save you. (Since we're coming, maybe we'll even bring some of our T-shirts and toothbrushes to hand out!) Someone from our staff may even stay for a couple weeks to teach you how to do church or children's ministry or a building project. Our missionaries will move in to show you how to start Bible studies, churches, and seminaries. We act as if we've cracked the code and figured out how to "do church."

Isn't that what our traditional missions model looks like and sounds like? Isn't that what we communicate to the global church? To make matters worse, this model isn't reserved for church. We think we've got all kinds of things figured out. We'll be over soon to show you how to dig wells, start schools, care for the sick, help the poor and even brush your teeth. We've got all that stuff figured out. Here we come to save the day!

White Man's Grave, a novel by Richard Dooling, is set in Sierra Leone. The main character is a visiting westerner who, like many, feels a sense of urgency to fix everything that he perceives is broken in the African culture. In a rare moment of confrontation, his African host says,

> That's when white people are most dangerous. When they try to make things 'better' for Africans . . . When white people come in with a lot of money or 'know-how' and try to make things 'better,' that's when things go to hell. Why can't white people just visit? Why must they always meddle? It's as if you were invited to dinner at someone's

house, and during your brief visit, you insisted on rearranging all the furniture in the house to suit your tastes.

I fear that the African host's brilliant example perfectly captures the way we approach global engagement. We come to visit and then start rearranging everything to suit our preferences. This needs to stop. We need to find a better way. We need to build a better model. Or maybe we just need to return to the model that the Apostle Paul laid out two thousand years ago.

In his first letter to the Christ-followers in Corinth, the Apostle Paul used a vivid word picture to explain how the growing movement of believers should act and interact. In 1 Corinthians 12, Paul compares the Church to a human body, a perfect blend of unity and diversity, and a memorable example of how we should interact with our brothers and sisters in Christ:

> Just as a body, though one, has many parts, but all its many parts form one body, so it is with Christ. For we were all baptized by one Spirit so as to form one body—whether Jews or Gentiles, slave or free—and we were all given the one Spirit to drink. Even so the body is not made up of one part but of many. (1 Corinthians 12:12-14)

Every body has unity (one body) as well as unbelievable diversity (many parts). The Church should be no different. It should be unified but not uniform. Unity shouldn't lead to sameness. On the contrary, there should be uniqueness and diversity within the Body. Paul is quite clear on this point:

> Now if the foot should say, "Because I am not a hand, I do not belong to the body," it would not for that reason stop being part of the body. And if the ear should say, "Because I am not an eye, I do not belong to the body," it would not for that reason stop being part of the body. if

the whole body were an eye, where would the sense of hearing be? If the whole body were an ear, where would the sense of smell be? But in fact God has placed the parts in the body, every one of them, just as he wanted them to be. If they were all one part, where would the body be? As it is, there are many parts, but one body.
(1 Corinthians 12:15-20)

Don't Underestimate Their Role

When I was in college, I was cast as a supporting character in two theatrical productions. Each actor was given a script with the words we were supposed to recite, but nothing more. We had to figure out the motivation – the thoughts and feelings behind the words. Let's do the same thing with the passage we just read. Imagine you are an actor playing the role of the Foot or the Ear. Take a moment to study your line. (Sorry. You don't really have a big speaking part.)

> **Foot:** *Because I am not a hand, I do not belong to the body.*
> **Ear:** *Because I am not an eye, I do not belong to the body.*

What's behind those comments? What is this character feeling? What is he or she thinking? It seems like these comments would be made in a melancholy tone, doesn't it? There's not a lot of pep or excitement here. There's discouragement and inferiority. There's a feeling of worthlessness and lots of self-doubt. The Foot and the Ear are ready to conclude that they don't belong to the body simply because they don't feel like they play a central role.

They're mistaken though. They are valuable - irreplaceable even! Their contribution is absolutely necessary. Our physical bodies demonstrate the necessity of diversity. We need our feet to function like feet and our ears to function like ears. We need all our parts to play their parts! God has situated each of the parts of the body just as He wants them to be. He's done the same with His Body, the Church. If we could draw one simple instruction from this idea, it's this: *Don't underestimate your part in the body.* No part of the Church is disposable or worthless. Some segments may seem weaker and unnecessary but, in reality, they are specifically designed by God to play a unique role in the Body.

Walking in Romania

I wish I had shared that message with the believers I met in a small Romanian village. Their church was not well resourced, seemingly frail and weak. They didn't have a separate building or any real programs of which to speak. Just a small group (mostly women) gathered in one of their homes, singing, crying and listening to God. Pastor Ioan Serb, a godly, loyal pastor visits them and several other similar churches, and encourages them in their spiritual formation.

I can imagine these brothers and sisters being tempted to underestimate their role. I'm afraid they may start to think that *"because I am not an eye, I do not belong to the body."* I hope that thought never crosses their minds. They most certainly do belong to the Body. And the rest of the Body needs what they have to offer: their depth of character, the strength of their faith, and their fervency in prayer. These qualities reveal a significant spiritual maturity. God has gifted and positioned the Romanian parts of His Body just as He wants them. I hope they don't underestimate their role. I hope we don't interact with them in ways that would undermine their role. I hope they know that they are an irreplaceable part of the Body.

Beyond Romania, many parts of our global Body need to hear this message. Far too many of our brothers and sisters have been treated as though they are not valuable parts of the Body of Christ. Isn't that the message we send when we transplant our methods, our money, and our programs into their communities? If Paul were writing to modern-day churches, he would make sure that the village churches in eastern Europe and the house churches in southeast Asia and the outdoor churches throughout sub-Saharan Africa and the host of other seemingly small and poor global churches could hear this message: *"You are an essential part of the Body of Christ! You have been specifically designed by God to play a role that no one else can play. Your uniqueness is intentional. Your contribution is invaluable. Don't let anyone convince you otherwise. You hold an irreplaceable position in the global Church. Don't underestimate your part in the Body."*

Don't Overestimate Our Role

There is another valuable lesson built into the body metaphor.

> The eye cannot say to the hand, "I don't need you!" And the head cannot say to the feet, "I don't need you!" On the contrary, those parts of the body that seem to be weaker are indispensable . . . (1 Corinthians 12:21-22)

Now that you've had some practice with script reading and characterization, take another shot at figuring out the motivation behind the statements these characters are making.

> **Eye** (speaking to the hand): *"I don't need you!"*
> **Head** (speaking to the feet): *"I don't need you!"*

It's not hard to figure out what the Eye or the Head think about themselves. These guys don't candy-coat how they feel. They let us know in no uncertain terms that they're all set. They don't need any help or input from anybody. They've got it all figured out. There's an unmistakable arrogance behind their words, *"I don't need you!"* It doesn't take an anatomy & physiology teacher to realize that the Eye and the Head are mistaken. They may think that they don't need the Feet or the Hands, but they are wrong. Anyone who's stubbed her toe or even gotten a hangnail will tell you that every bit of the body is connected and significant. To be complete, whole, and fully functional, we need every part playing its part. The Head and the Eye need to get a clue and learn a lesson; namely: *Don't overestimate your part in the Body.*

Walking in South Africa

The American Church tends to overestimate our role in the Body. This became unmistakably clear to me on a trip to South Africa. A team from my church was visiting and working with a missionary family who had planted a church there. Our team was one of many that had been scheduled to be part of a church construction program. Over the course of several months, materials and teams were sent over from the United States. An American missions agency, it's staff, and volunteers took care of the entire build. Our team was the last one working on the project. We laid tile, sanded doors and essentially finished the construction before heading back to the States. In the weeks that followed, I interacted with the American missionary who had hosted our team. In one of our e-mail exchanges, we talked about church programs and services, specifically communion. I wondered if there was anything unique or culturally specific about the way they engaged in this sacred moment. His reply was unforgettable. He wrote something to this effect, "We don't really do anything different than how you would do it in the States. In fact, we had our home church send us the golden communion trays and the little plastic communion cups so we could administer communion each month."

Seriously? What must that have communicated to our brothers and sisters in South Africa? *"We've got this all figured out. We know the way to build church buildings. We'll send the teams, the tools and the supplies. We'll even send the laborers to build a nice American-style church for you. But wait! There's more. We've also discovered the way to participate in the Lord's Supper. We have the right trays. We have the little cups. Hang on. We'll get you some so that you can participate in communion too!"* It breaks my heart to think that there is a group of Christ-followers in South Africa who are essentially being told, *"We don't need you."*

Don't Stop at Verse Eleven

The American church has gotten really good at overestimating our role and communicating our arrogance to our brothers and sisters around the world. As we explored in chapter three, we've built our entire missions model on an inflated view of ourselves. It's as though we read Romans 1:11, but failed to read verse twelve.

Before he visited the believers in Rome, the Apostle Paul wrote a letter to them to give a preview of his visit and his teaching. Early on in the letter Paul told his readers what he was hoping for from his visit. He said, "I long to see you so that I may impart to you some spiritual gift to make you strong . . ." (Romans 1:11)

Paul had been given a spiritual gift that he wanted to share with the believers in Rome. He had something welling up inside him that he wanted to spill out onto those Christians. What Paul expressed in verse eleven captures the sentiment of many of us who are eager to engage in some kind of global ministry. We have received something worth sharing, and we want to venture cross-culturally to share it.

Think of all the ways we've embodied this idea. We have construction skills and want to offer those to make others strong. We have evangelistic passion and want to offer that to make churches strong. We have a great children's curriculum and are ready to offer that to make families strong. We have hearts full of compassion and want to offer care to make the weak strong. Most missionaries could use a slight variation of verse eleven to sum up their motivation for cross-cultural ministry. *"I can't wait to go to _____ , so I can _____."*

50

Unfortunately, we tend to stop at verse eleven. You will notice that Paul did not. After explaining that he had something he wanted to share with the believers in Rome, he seems to qualify or complete that thought. It's as if his words didn't quite come out right, and he wants to take another stab at accurately capturing his motivation. So in verse twelve, he says, "— that is, that you and I may be mutually encouraged by each other's faith."

That clarification paints quite a different picture. This is not the same as us offering something that we have to those people who don't have enough. Verse eleven, taken by itself, could imply a one-way flow of resources and a one-sided arrangement. But according to verse twelve, Paul didn't envision a one-way relationship at all. He was not imagining a scenario where he shared his spiritual gifts with the poor and needy people in Rome and then headed back to Antioch. He didn't foresee a relationship between the "Haves" and the "Have Nots." Rather, he imagined a two-way, mutual, reciprocal relationship where both he and the Roman believers would be involved in give-and-take. Yes, he had things to share with them that would strengthen and encourage them, but he was also looking forward to learning and growing from what they had to offer him. Both sides would be mutually encouraged by each other's faith!

We do really well with verse eleven. All the missionaries I know do their very best to impart to others some spiritual gifts to make them strong. This is admirable but incomplete. Paul points to the value and necessity of true partnership. Our global engagement needs to be built on both giving and receiving. We seem to have lost this. We seem to ignore the fact that God's people around the globe have spiritual gifts to share with us. We have too often convinced ourselves that we have something to offer, but nothing to learn; plenty to give but no need to receive. We've gotten hung up on verse eleven and hung up on ourselves.

It's easy to think that God wants to use our global outreach efforts to bring revival to the rest of the world. *Could it be that God wants to use our global engagement to revive us?* Sure, we have spiritual gifts to offer others. But think of all we could learn from the global church about prayer, faith, perseverance, persecution, compassion and community. We really don't have to look too hard to recognize that the Western church is sadly lacking in many of these essential spiritual virtues. An arm-in-arm partnership with God's people across the globe could be the very thing He uses to transform us into the people He wants us to be. But first we need to embrace Romans 1:12, recognizing that we aren't starting this work and we are not at the center of this work. We're simply one part of God's global family learning to walk with Him and walk with others down the path of partnership so we and our global partners can be *"mutually encouraged by each other's faith."*

A New Model for Global Engagement

What does it look like to replace the "West to the Rest" model with a new one? What if we take the principles from 1 Corinthians 12 and Romans 1 and turn them into a picture? The result is a model that looks something like this:

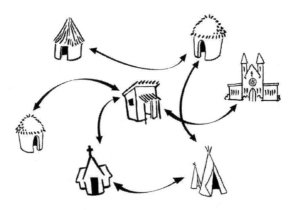

For me, this picture captures a powerful mental image. What if we move toward that kind of engagement? What if we stop acting as if we are the savior and instead embodied the humility of our Savior? What if, rather than showing up and starting something new, we join what God is already doing, affirming and encouraging national believers, and leaning into their wisdom and assets? What if we continue to bring our strengths and gifts and resources yet also fully expect to receive from the strengths and gifts and resources of our global brothers and sisters? That is such a beautiful vision of the global Church, each part maintaining its diversity while also embracing unity. Brothers and sisters in Christ from all corners of the world walking together, mutually encouraged by each other's faith!

Learning to Walk Together

Several years ago, our church decided to explore this new model for global engagement. We knew we shouldn't dismantle or immediately replace the existing model, but we wanted to start something new alongside our traditional approach. So in addition to supporting missionaries around the world, we started to build relationships with indigenous leaders who were sparking transformation in their communities. We asked them to point out what God was doing in and through them and offered to help however we could. Like Philip stepping into the chariot, we wanted to identify what God was already doing and then see if we could support that in any way. Simply put, we wanted to *go where God was leading and join what God was doing*.

In some cases, we formed relationships directly with national churches and leaders. In other situations, we worked with a like-minded agency to help us make those connections and build those bridges. That first option (direct church-to-church connection without the support of another agency) has become increasingly difficult because of international tension and security. Forging those relationship – and specifically transferring funds – without the help of a global organization is not recommended. Thankfully, a new wave of mission agencies is rising up to enable churches to make these kinds of global connections. The very best organization we've found is The 410 Bridge, which is currently helping hundreds of churches cultivate healthy partnerships in several developing countries. Others include the Global Hope Network, who focuses on unreached people groups; She Is Safe, who advocates for and empowers women and girls; and the Slavic Gospel Association, who works throughout Russia.

With the help of The 410 Bridge, our church set out on the path of partnership. We began by acknowledging that we were not the first ones on the path. We were entering countries and cultures where God and His people were already on the move. Rather than getting to work on projects, we got to work on relationships – walking alongside, talking and praying with our brothers and sisters. We wanted to know them and learn what God was doing in their midst. We wanted them to know us and learn what God was doing in our community. We committed to walking with each other, allowing the relationship to pave the way forward. We truly believed that any results we achieved would be the fruit of these relationships.

You may need to make that shift as well. It may be time to think less about results and more about relationships, less about global projects and more about global partners, less about starting something new and more about joining what God is already doing. If those ideas sound inspiring, then start down that path. Develop and nurture some global connections. Discover some of what God is doing around the world. Ask questions. Listen. Pray together. Walk together. Recognize that you are not the first one on the path; God is already on the move. Walk with Him and with His people.

If you're a pastor or church leader, now is the time to lead your church down this path. You have a role to play in opening people's eyes to God's global work and reminding others that we are one part of a global Body. Here are a few tips and trail markers that may help you move down the path of partnership.

Slow Down: There are no quick fixes in global partnership. There are no "one and done" projects. It's not about doing a global adventure once in your life; it's about making global relationships a part of your life. Walking side-by-side, arm-in-arm (or in many African cultures, hand-in-hand!) together for the long-term. There's no real hurry. It's more about the journey than the destination. Slow down. This isn't a race; it's a walk.

Keep Moving: We're not building a monument; we're part of a movement. Walking is active, not passive. Don't settle for the sidelines. Get in the game and stay in the game. Don't stop just because it gets challenging or other matters become more urgent. Global partnerships never seem urgent, but they are critically important if we are to be the people of God we were created to be and play the role we were designed to play. It will be difficult and costly. You may have to adjust your pace from time to time, but don't stop walking. Keep moving.

Learn As You Go: Isn't that the beauty of walking? It's something we can learn. You didn't used to know how to do it. You didn't do it perfectly at first. You started slowly. You took one step before you fell and had to start again. You staggered and stumbled and had the bumps and bruises to prove it. But you learned along the way. Global partnerships are no different. They don't come naturally. We won't do them perfectly. But we'll get better over time if we learn as we go, keep moving, and slow down.

Walking Together as a Global Body

Oscar Muriu, pastor of The Nairobi Chapel, reworded Paul's instructions to the first-century church. Though not inspired, Muriu's words are certainly what the 21st century church needs to hear.

> Now the body is not made up of one part but of many. If the American church should say, "Because I am not an African, I do not belong to the body," it would not for that reason cease to be part of the body. And if the European church should say, "Because I am not an Asian, I do no belong to the body," it would not for that reason cease to be part of the body.

> If the whole body were German, where would the sense of vibrancy be? If the whole body were a European, where would the sense of color be? But in fact God has arranged the parts in the body, every one of them, just as He wanted them to be. If they were all one part, where would the body be? As it is, there are many parts, but one body.

> The American church cannot say to the Asian Church, "I don't need you!" And the European Church cannot say to the African church, "I don't need you!" On the contrary, the Asian parts that seem to be weaker are indispensable, and the African parts that we think are less honorable should be treated with special honor. And the Latin American parts that seem unpresentable are treated with special modesty, while the presentable parts like the big and wealthy American church need no special treatment. But God has combined the members of the body and has given greater honor to the parts that lacked it, so that there should be no division in the body, but that its parts should have equal concern for each other. If one part suffers,

every part suffers with it; if one part is honored, every part rejoices with it. Now you are the body of Christ, and each one of you is a part of it.

Don't underestimate the role of your brothers and sisters in Christ. They were designed by God to play a valuable and irreplaceable part in His global Body. They desperately need to hear that affirmation, and I think they should hear it from us in the West.

Don't overestimate your role. You are part of something much bigger, and you'll miss out on what God is doing if you're not open to contributions from the rest of the Body. American believers desperately need to embrace this kind of humility and begin to live it out when we interact globally.

Don't stop at verse eleven. Yes, you have something to offer. But you also have much to learn. When all the parts of the Body work and walk together, we are mutually encouraged by each other's faith. We discover a beautiful, world-changing preview of God's coming Kingdom. Walking together, we are better able to see and seize the divine opportunities that God has prepared for us. Arm-in-arm, we are able to move off the sidelines and into the world-redeeming action that God is orchestrating. Walking together is the best way to engage in global ministry.

But where should we be going together? What paths should we and our partners walk down? What ground should we be gaining? What fights should we be fighting? Those are the questions we'll address in the next chapter.

START WALKING
Notes and Next Step

Walk This Way: How?
- Don't underestimate their role.
- Don't overestimate our role.
- Slow down, keep moving, and learn as you go.

Next Steps
Oscar Muriu is one of the first international leaders to help the American church understand healthy partnership. His archived talks from URBANA and the Global Leadership Summit are rich and inspiring. The interview he gave with Leadership Journal is insightful and eye-opening. You can find a link to the transcript at www.WalkThisWay.world.

6 THE THREE PATHS GOD IS MOVING DOWN

We act as if God is healing only some of our brokenness.
In reality, He is restoring all that has been lost.

God does good work – very good work. He said so Himself when He finished the work of creation. Check out this familiar passage from Genesis 1:28-31:

> God blessed [Adam and Eve] and said to them, "Be fruitful and increase in number; fill the earth and subdue it. Rule over the fish in the sea and the birds in the sky and over every living creature that moves on the ground." God saw all that he had made, and it was very good.

Everything was perfect. Everything was right. There was nothing but harmony, unity and peace in three key relationships. First, Adam and Eve experienced peace and perfection in their *relationship with God*. There was no guilt, no hiding, no distance between God and mankind. Second, Adam and Eve experienced unity in their *relationship with each other*. There was no interpersonal conflict. They were unique and distinct, yet they were unified and complimentary. They had a whole and beautiful relationship with each other. Third, there was perfect harmony in the *relationship between mankind and the rest of creation.* Mankind was given responsibility to cultivate and care for the natural world. There was a good working relationship within creation. The land yielded what it was supposed to yield. Plants and animals grew, developed, acted and interacted according to their design. Adam and Eve nurtured and stewarded the elements of creation. Mankind's three key relationships – with God, with others, and with the rest of creation – were perfect and complete. There was spiritual, physical and social harmony, for a while at least.

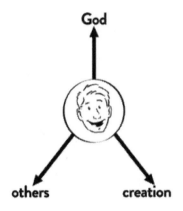

Three Broken Relationships

Everything broke when Adam and Eve turned their backs on God. Their rebellion affected all three of the relationships that had once been perfect. Genesis 3:8 highlights the first layer of destruction. "The man and his wife heard the sound of the LORD God as he was walking in the garden in the cool of the day, and they hid from the LORD God among the trees of the garden."

Instead of walking and talking with God, Adam and Eve hid from Him. Trust was replaced by fear. The connection between mankind and God, a relationship that used to be whole, was now broken. That's not the only relationship that suffered. When Adam finally came out of hiding and began to talk to God again, it was obvious that something else had shifted. Adam's relationship with Eve was not what it had been. God asked a simple question. Adam was quick to point fingers. Genesis 3:12 says, "The man said, 'The woman you put here with me – she gave me some fruit from the tree, and I ate it.'"

Unity, intimacy, and love were gone, replaced by contention, stress, and blame. Adam and Eve's relationship with each other, a relationship that was once so beautiful, had turned ugly.

Sadly, there's still more brokenness to be found in this story. As He spoke with Adam and Eve, God explained how sin had ruined yet another relationship.

> Cursed is the ground because of you; through painful toil you will eat food from it all the days of your life. It will produce thorns and thistles for you, and you will eat the plants of the field. By the sweat of your brow you will eat your food until you return to the ground, since from it you were taken; for dust you are and to dust you will return. (Genesis 3:17-19)

The created order wasn't orderly any more. Working the ground became difficult. Stewarding the elements of creation became more complicated. The physical world itself now groans and heaves under the weight of sin. Paradise has been lost. And with that, the trilogy of brokenness is complete. Our three core relationships have been shattered by sin. Consequently, we now live in a world of *spiritual*, *physical* and *social* brokenness.

In their best-selling book, *When Helping Hurts*, Brain Fikkert and Steve Corbett summarize the brokenness this way:

Of course, the grand story of Scripture does not end with creation. Adam and Eve disobeyed God, and their hearts were darkened. The Genesis account records that all of Adam and Eve's relationships immediately became distorted: their relationship with God was damaged, as their intimacy with Him was replaced with fear; their relationship with others was broken, as Adam quickly blamed Eve for their sin; and their relationship with the rest of creation became distorted, as God cursed the ground.

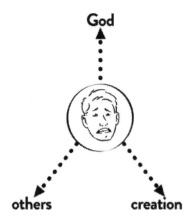

Look around. Look in the mirror. You don't need someone to tell you this; the three-fold wreckage is obvious and undeniable. The human race is clearly not in right relationship with God. We're searching, restless, and separated from Him. And that's not the only separation we feel. We're separated from one another as well. The innocence is gone. We're guarded and suspicious, isolated and lonely. When we do interact with each other, it's far too easy for us to use and manipulate and oppress one another.

The oppression isn't only person-to-person. Creation itself has been oppressed. We're not seeing the same balance and harmony in

THE THREE PATHS GOD IS MOVING DOWN

the natural world that Adam and Eve once experienced. There are droughts and famines, diseases and plagues. Everything is fractured – our relationship with God, our relationship with each other and our relationship with the rest of creation. That brokenness has been our reality since Genesis 3. That's the world we live in today, and that's the world Jesus stepped into when He arrived.

Jesus Heals All That's Broken

The generations between Adam and Jesus lived and breathed the brokenness that was introduced in the garden. They searched in vain for ways to restore what had been lost, but the separation was too great. The only glimpses of hope came from the lips of Israel's prophets. They spoke of a Messiah, a Savior who would one day come to mend what had been torn apart. Finally, that long-awaited day arrived. Luke recounts the momentous occasion in Luke 4:14-21:

> Jesus returned to Galilee in the power of the Spirit, and news about him spread through the whole countryside. He was teaching in their synagogues, and everyone praised him. He went to Nazareth, where he had been brought up, and on the Sabbath day he went into the synagogue, as was his custom.

There is a sense of anticipation in those words. There's a fresh feeling in the air. Something big is on the horizon. Jesus had been away from his home and his family. He had fasted and prayed for over a month. He had just been baptized by John and publically affirmed by God the Father. Then He returned to Galilee, to his hometown of Nazareth.

Think about a daughter returning home after being away at college or a son coming back to his neighborhood after boot camp. There's excitement and eagerness. She's all grown up. He's become a man. A lot has changed; a lot more is about to change.

Jesus didn't go to his parents' house, nor did He make his way to his dad's carpentry shop. He didn't find his old school or the field where He used to play. Instead, He went to the synagogue, the center of God's activity. He arrived on the Sabbath, the holy day. Something big was about to happen. In Luke 4:16-21, we see that something new was about to begin.

> Jesus stood up to read, and the scroll of the prophet Isaiah was handed to him. Unrolling it, he found the place where it is written: "The Spirit of the Lord is on me, because he has anointed me to proclaim good news to the poor. He has sent me to proclaim freedom for the prisoners and recovery of sight for the blind, to set the oppressed free, to proclaim the year of the Lord's favor."
>
> Then he rolled up the scroll, gave it back to the attendant and sat down. The eyes of everyone in the synagogue were fastened on him. He began by saying to them, "Today this scripture is fulfilled in your hearing."

Of all the things Jesus could have read from the thirty-seven books of law, history, and prophecy, He read Isaiah's seven hundred-year-old description of the coming Messiah. No other Scripture was a better introduction. Isaiah's words provided the perfect prelude to Jesus' life work, the perfect launch pad for His mission.

The words Jesus read came from Isaiah 61 and pointed to a day when the Messiah would restore all that had been lost. He picked up the scroll and essentially said, "I'm that guy! I'm the One, the Messiah. I've come to offer hope in spite of all that's been broken. I've come to restore everything that sin has shattered."

Richard Stearns captured these ideas so well in his best-selling book titled *The Hole in Our Gospel*. He points out that just as sin destroyed our three core relationships, Jesus came to heal those three core relationships.

Healing Our Relationship with God

According to Isaiah 61 and Luke 4, the Messiah would devote Himself to *proclamation*. He came to . . .

- Proclaim good news (Luke 4:18).
- Proclaim freedom (Luke 4:18).
- Proclaim the year of the Lord's favor (Luke 4:19).

Jesus came to proclaim. He had a message to share. Grace can replace judgment. Instead of bondage, there can be freedom. Forgiveness and redemption are available. The relationship with God that is broken can be made whole! Jesus came to announce, preach, declare, and proclaim that life-changing good news.

Healing Our Relationship with the Rest of Creation

As well as proclamation, the Messiah's life would also be marked by *compassion*. Luke's summary offers a glimpse of this. Isaiah's original prophecy makes it unmistakable. The Messiah will . . .

- Bring recovery of sight for the blind (Luke 4:18).
- Bind up the brokenhearted (Isaiah 61:1).
- Comfort all who mourn (Isaiah 61:2).
- Provide for those who grieve (Isaiah 61:3).

Jesus didn't just talk; He acted. More specifically, He cured the diseased, showed empathy for the poor, fed the hungry, and healed the disabled. In other words, He didn't just address their spiritual brokenness but their physical brokenness as well. He reached down with compassion to those who had been beaten down by this broken world.

Healing Our Relationship with Each Other

Both proclamation and compassion would shape Jesus' life and direct His steps. Isaiah spoke about one more pursuit that would also drive the Messiah. He would have an unwavering commitment to *justice*. The prophecy speaks of . . .

- Freedom for the prisoners (Luke 4:18).
- Release for the captives (Isaiah 61:1).
- Setting the oppressed free (Luke 4:18).
- Proclaiming the year of the Lord's favor (Luke 4:19).

Jesus would speak for those who couldn't speak for themselves. He would stand up for those who couldn't stand up for themselves. He would be the Advocate for the mistreated and the Hero for the underdog. He would be the One to bring justice when our relationships with each other become distorted and oppressive.

Isaiah's prophecy refers to "the year of the LORD's favor." This is a reference to Israel's Year of Jubilee, a fantastic practice that God prescribed in Leviticus 25. The Year of Jubilee was commanded to take place every 50 years (basically once a generation). At that time, God's people were called to level the playing field. Slaves would be set free, debts would be forgiven, and all land would be returned to its original owners (the clans and tribes that had been given the property when Israel entered the Promised Land). The Year of Jubilee was a chance to hit the reset button. It was God's way of keeping the rich from getting too rich, the poor from getting too poor, the strong from getting too strong and the weak from getting too weak. The Year of Jubilee was established to ensure that socioeconomic gaps didn't continue to widen.

Incidentally, many domestic and global economists believe that this widening gap – specifically between the rich and the poor – is *the* key issue that must be addressed in developing countries. Anyone who has travelled internationally has noticed the gap between the "Haves" and the "Have Nots." That chasm has terrible ripple effects. A practice like the Year of Jubilee would have diminished those effects for ancient Israel. Jesus, the Messiah Isaiah prophesied, came to offer that kind of harmony and justice.

Compassion and Justice

Jesus' mission to heal all that's been broken opens our eyes to the important distinction between *compassion* and *justice*. Compassion is needed because our relationships with the rest of creation have been broken. Justice is needed because our relationships with each other have been broken. Let's explore that a bit further.

Compassion: Many of the challenges and hardships that people face are not necessarily someone's fault. They are simply the result of a world that is crumbling under the weight of sin. There are droughts, thirst, famines and hunger. There is sickness, deformity, disease and plagues. We cannot pin the blame for these things on a particular person. They are the result of a broken relationship between humanity and the created world. Situations like these call for compassion. People have been beaten up and knocked down by a fallen world. They need care from someone who will reach out with hands of *compassion*.

Justice: Some of the brokenness that we face is someone's fault. People with power use and abuse their power in order to use and abuse other people. Oppression follows. Violence results. The poor and vulnerable are enslaved. Situations like these call for more than compassion; they demand *justice*. Seeing the distinction between compassion and justice enables us to address the different kinds of brokenness more effectively.

Jesus' Followers Heal All That's Broken

Seven centuries before Jesus' birth, God's people were far from Him, far from their Promised Land, and far from living in harmony with each other. Into that context, Isaiah spoke of a Messiah who would one day offer three-fold restoration and hope. First, He would be committed to proclamation, speaking out with words of forgiveness. Second, He would be known by compassion, reaching down with hands of love. Third, He would be marked by justice, standing up for those who were oppressed. This is how we would recognize the Messiah. He would address all the pain that the human race was feeling in the spiritual, physical and social realms.

It should come as no surprise that Jesus' followers are expected to follow Jesus. If He is going down paths of proclamation, compassion and justice, then His people ought to be going those directions as well. That expectation is nothing new; it's as old as Isaiah's seven hundred-year old prophecy. Another one of Israel's prophets, Micah, had been just as clear as Isaiah had been. Isaiah, as we've seen, described what the Messiah's life would look like. Micah described what the lives of the people of God should look like. One of Micah's messages was so simple, clear and straightforward. In just fourteen words, he captured exactly what God expects from His people:

> He has shown you, O man, what is good. And what does the LORD require of you? *To act justly and to love mercy and to walk humbly with your God.* (Micah 6:8, italics added)

There it is. Plain and simple. God expects us to *walk humbly* with Him, receiving His forgiveness and proclaiming to the world through our words and actions that mankind can be reconciled to God. That's not all. God also expects us to *love mercy*, to reach out hands of compassion, to care for those who are hurting and sick, and to love those who have been knocked down by this broken world. Finally, God expects us to *act justly*, to advocate for the oppressed, to speak up and stand up for those who cannot, and to bring hope and justice to those who have none. Through Micah, God calls His people to be people in right relationship with Him, in right relationship with the rest of creation and in right relationship with others. Just as Isaiah did, Micah recognized what was broken and in need of restoration. All three of our core relationships have been broken. God, through Jesus and His followers, has set out to restore all those relationships.

- Proclamation is speaking out because people have been separated from God.
- Compassion is reaching down because people have been beaten down by this world.
- Justice is stepping up because people have been beaten up by others.

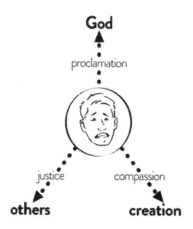

Walking Three Paths

To be the people God is calling us to be – men and women who are truly following Jesus – we must follow Him wherever He leads. We need to move down the same path that He is moving down. We must live lives of proclamation, helping people see and hear the good news. Billions are separated from Him. We can point them to the One who can bridge that gap. We can introduce them to Jesus and the forgiveness and life that He alone offers. And we can partner with the people of God across the globe that are doing this in their communities. We can come alongside local pastors and teachers. We can support national church plants and training schools. We can facilitate Bible translation and distribution. We can – and we must – be involved in the proclamation of the good news.

But we can't stop there. A one-legged stool isn't going to stand. Our lives must also be filled with compassion. The people of God should move out of places of comfort, out of their homes, and out of their churches and move toward the hurting, offering help and hope. True followers of Christ will live with their eyes open to the needs around them, their hearts awakened to the brokenness of this world, and their hands extended with care and grace. We must walk down this path and we'd be wise to walk with global believers who are doing likewise. All over the world, men and women of God are reaching down with compassion and making a tangible difference in their villages: bringing clean water, improving the quality of education, offering medical care, creating jobs and stimulating economic development. They are showing compassion in these and so many other ways. Let's join them on that path.

A third pursuit must mark our lives as well. We must be people of justice. We must be the ones who run in when everyone else runs out. We must be the ones who remind the abused and the oppressed that God is not absent. Even in the darkest places on this planet, our advocacy and presence should proclaim, *"Surely the LORD is in this place."* He is not blind to their suffering or deaf to their cries. And we, His people, are not content to stand by – safe, isolated, and far too busy with our own lives – while men and women, boys and girls, each made in the image of God, are bought, beaten, sold and enslaved. Not on our watch! If we are truly following Jesus, we will be the ones to stand up for justice.

Some of us may have opportunities to be on the frontlines of this fight. All of us have the opportunity to engage in the fight. That begins when we examine our lives and open our eyes to the possibility that our choices may be contributing to the mistreatment of others. Believe it or not, the products we purchase and the lifestyle we choose to live could foster injustice and enable slavery. We need to be aware and intentional. Thankfully, we're not on our own. By partnering with organizations like International Justice Mission, She is Safe, and the Restavek Freedom Foundation, our church has been able to seek and pursue justice in the global communities where we serve. Coming alongside those organizations, or others like them, may be just the step you need to take to follow Jesus down the path of justice.

God is on the move, not just here and there but everywhere. He is offering restoration, not just for some of the brokenness but for all of the brokenness. We're called to follow Him down the paths of proclamation, compassion, and justice, offering hope and healing to those who are separated from God, oppressed by this broken world and mistreated by one another. As we move down these paths, we offer a glimpse of the coming Kingdom. Just as Jesus did, we foreshadow a day when He will make all things new and fully restore all that has been lost. From now until then, the people of God must simply follow Him as we *speak out*, *reach down*, and *stand up*. It's what we do.

What we do is important. So is *how* we do it. As we move down these three paths with our global partners, we need to walk wisely. We must choose our steps carefully. We will do well to commit ourselves to walking according to the five best practices outlined in the following chapter.

START WALKING
Notes and Next Steps

Walk This Way: What?
- Speak out in proclamation.
- Reach down with compassion.
- Stand up for justice.

Next Steps
- Years ago, Richard Stearns opened our eyes to *The Hole in Our Gospel*. More recently, he's reminded us that the task of filling the hole is still *Unfinished*. Both of these books urge us to join God in all the restoration He is pursuing.
- Join the fight for justice by partnering with **International Justice Mission, Restavek Freedom Foundation** or **She is Safe**.
- To view a presentation of the content in this chapter, check out the video *Until Then* on www.WalkThisWay.world.

7 A MONKEY, A FISH,
AND FIVE BEST PRACTICES

We assure ourselves that good intentions are enough.
The fact of the matter is that we need to engage in wise action.

"It's the thought that counts, right?" We've all heard and probably used that expression. When someone's well-intended actions don't quite pan out as hoped, we like to use this good-natured excuse. In his book *Cross-Cultural Servanthood,* Duane Elmer shares a fascinating parable that sheds light on this question. See if it sounds familiar.

> A typhoon had temporarily stranded a monkey on an island. In a secure, protected place, while waiting for the raging waters to recede, he spotted a fish swimming against the current. It seemed obvious to the monkey that the fish was struggling and in need of assistance. Being of kind heart, the monkey resolved to help the fish.
> A tree precariously dangled over the very spot where the fish seemed to be struggling. At considerable risk to himself, the monkey moved far out on a limb, reached down and snatched the fish from the threatening waters. Immediately scurrying back to the safety of his shelter, he carefully laid the fish on dry ground. For a few moments

the fish showed excitement, but soon settled into a peaceful rest. Joy and satisfaction swelled inside the monkey. He had successfully helped another creature.

It's such a silly story, but doesn't it perfectly capture the way we far too often approach situations? We mean well but act foolishly. This is especially true in our global interactions. The world is littered with examples of well-meaning outsiders acting like that monkey. It takes more than good intentions; it takes wise action.

In previous chapters, we've explored well-intended, but foolish actions. It's time to turn a corner and discover what a better path looks like. What follows are five best practices to help us channel our good intentions for global engagement into wise actions. Before exploring each one, here's a glimpse of all five:

- Long-Term Rather Than Short-Term
- Do With Rather Than Do For
- Build Capacity Rather Than Create Dependency
- Empower Leaders Rather Than Meet Needs
- Focused Rather Than Scattered

Long-Term Rather Than Short-Term

On a recent trip to Kenya, I shared some Psalms with our team during our daily debrief. One thought led to another and, before we knew it, we began to see an eye-opening theme. Take a look.

- I will perpetuate your memory through all generations; therefore the nations will praise you forever and ever. (Psalm 45:17)
- For the Lord is good and his love endures forever; his faithfulness continues through all generations. (Psalm 100:5)
- Your faithfulness continues through all generations; you established the earth, and it endures. (Psalm 119:90)

74

- Your kingdom is an everlasting kingdom,
  and your dominion endures through all generations.
  (Psalm 145:13)

As we considered these (and other) passages and rehearsed what we were experiencing in this rural, Kenyan village, we made an interesting observation: God seems to measure time not in minutes or months, but in generations. His involvement stretches from eternity past and continues into eternity future. He's clearly a God of long-term involvement and impact; most American missions projects are not. They tend to be short-term and shortsighted. We want to have an immediate impact and quickly see measurable results so we lean toward relief rather than development. We tend to focus on projects in place of people and on results instead of relationships. It's so easy, even with the best of intentions, to get caught up in short-term programs rather than long-term partnership. Here's one example from my church's experience.

Early on in our partnership with the leaders in Karogoto, Kenya, several different people suggested similar ideas. Big-hearted members of our church, wanting to alleviate some of the challenges our partners were facing, suggested that we collect a certain item and give it to our friends in Karogoto. People asked if we could collect T-shirts, shoes, toothbrushes, Bibles, tools, school supplies, soccer balls, oven mitts and more! The desire to help was always genuine; the passion was always high. We actually followed through with some of those ideas and organized some of the collections. At the time, it seemed like a good idea. Our gifts were received with gratitude, and we were filled with a sense of accomplishment and feelings of generosity. But some of us began to wonder if these gifts were actually helpful and if they were they making any kind of long-term difference.

Around the same time, our partners in Kenya proposed another kind of project. This one didn't involve shirts or shoes. It was all

75

about sweaters. In order to go to school, Kenyan students need their own school uniform sweater. That need sparked the opportunity for a local business of a knitting facility that would produce those sweaters locally, right in Karogoto. The local Leadership Council developed the concept. It was their vision, but they needed some help. If we could provide start-up capital, then they could acquire the knitting machines and train local women to knit the sweaters, which would then be sold to families in Karogoto and beyond.

That's exactly what happened! The Blessed Hands knitting facility started small, but has steadily grown and developed. Their chairwoman is pictured below holding their very first school uniform sweater!

Today they have their own workspace and storefront where 100 women find employment, making not just sweaters, but dresses, hats and scarves as well. I just returned from Karogoto, and, while I was there, I discovered that they've expanded their business to include beadwork, handbags, purses, necklaces and bracelets. It is an exciting and expanding business, and my daughters have the accessories to prove it!

I couldn't help but contrast this project with some of the ones we had initiated earlier. The differences went far beyond shirts verses sweaters. Rather, it was the difference between short-term versus long-term. The first projects provided one item (a shirt, a toothbrush, a backpack, etc.) to many of the residents in the community. That item seemed to meet an immediate need. But it was just one toothbrush. That gift is a short-term gift with a short-term impact. The school sweaters represented much more than that.

Establishing a knitting facility took a long time - a really long time. Initial contributions to the knitting facility didn't provide immediate help to anyone. Kids didn't get sweaters on the first day or even in the first year. The business wasn't profitable right from the start. All we had to show for our early contributions were a few knitting machines that only a few Karogoto residents even knew how to use. The project didn't have an immediate impact, but it certainly had a long-term one. Years later, Blessed Hands provides employment, clothing, and commerce for the entire community! The difference is significant. The first kind of project met what we perceived as an immediate need. The other started a process that could offer solutions for generations.

We learned a lot from those projects and experiences. One of the biggest lessons is that we would much rather focus our energy and effort on the long-term rather than the short-term. The ripple effects of that one shift are significant. For instance, following the wisdom of our national partners, we no longer give away shoes or T-shirts or toothbrushes or school supplies or whatever we well-intentioned Americans want to give away. Giving away stuff like that in the moment makes us feel better about ourselves but does nothing to address the long-term development of the community.

77

In fact, according to our partners, giving like this is almost always harmful. It undermines local leadership, discourages entrepreneurship, and creates a sense of entitlement. One of my Kenyan friends went so far as to say, "When you give stuff away like that, you turn my people into beggars!" That's obviously not what we want to happen! Instead, with our partners showing us how, we leverage our resources toward projects and opportunities that provide a long-term benefit to the community and make an impact that will hopefully last for generations.

Do With Rather Than Do For

The second principle is clearly related to the first. When you are interested in the long-term rather than the short-term, you'll find that doing a project *with* someone is much better than doing one *for* someone. It's the difference between relief (doing for people) and development (doing with people). No one has described this distinction better than Steve Corbett and Brian Fikkert in *When Helping Hurts*.

They explain that relief is needed in those relatively rare circumstances where people truly are helpless. For instance, when there's been a genuine crisis – an earthquake, a tsunami, or any type of sudden and unexpected catastrophe. In those situations, it's appropriate and genuinely helpful for people outside the situation to step in, take charge, and do for people what they cannot do for themselves. Stop the bleeding. Bring some structure. Restore some semblance of order. This is relief, and in those rare cases, it's the best route to take.

Development is different. Anyone involved in development recognizes that the vast majority of people are not helpless and shouldn't be treated as such. When you pursue development, you lean into the gifts, abilities, desires and assets that people already possess. Development is working *with* people as they move toward a better future. Development has a long-term focus, making a difference for generations.

It's easy to read about that distinction. It makes sense on paper, but for some reason, we have a really hard time making the shift from relief to development. Over and over again in one place after another, we step in, take charge, and do things *for* people who are quite capable of doing those very things for themselves. This approach (offering relief when development is needed) hasn't helped. In fact, it has done quite the opposite. Consider these observations from Bob Lupton's book *Toxic Charity*:

> Take Haiti, for example. No other country in the Western Hemisphere has received more charitable aid and services from governments and nonprofits. Yet its poverty and dysfunction continue to deepen. During the four decades prior to the devastating earthquake of January 2010, $8.3 billion in foreign aid flowed into Haiti. Yet the country has ended up 25 percent poorer than before the aid began. The current earthquake tragedy [of 2010] has ballooned additional aid commitments by another $9 billion from thirty-nine countries. But the prognosis for sustained improvement is no better today.

> "The problem is not goodwill," says anthropologist Timothy Schwartz, longtime Haiti resident who emailed from the midst of the earthquake devastation. "I don't even think the problem is resources . . . The big problem is lack of accountability, lack of a mechanism to pressure aid agencies into effective, long-term development." Schwartz has witnessed it all firsthand. Decades of free aid from well-meaning benefactors has produced an entitlement mentality and eroded a spirit of entrepreneurship and self-sufficiency. The outpouring of more aid, though necessary to preserve life in a time of disaster, is ultimately

worsening the underlying problem. Humanitarian responses unaccompanied by disciplined development strategies become a curse on a country.

Dambisa Moyo, in her bestselling exposé, *Dead Aid*, writes about assistance to her native Africa: "The reality is aid has helped make the poor poorer and growth slower. Aid has been, and continues to be, an unmitigated political, economic and humanitarian disaster for most parts of the developing world."

I realize that there are a host of other factors at play in Haiti and the countries in Africa that have received "dead aid." The results that we see in those places cannot be simply explained. I have no doubt that Lupton and Moyo would agree that these are extremely complex issues. Their central point is one we need to hear though: *Doing for people, rather than doing with people, is usually the wrong choice.* Granted, there are times when relief (aid) is necessary. In those moments of crisis, we should be ready to do whatever we can to help. But every other time we must have the wisdom and the discipline to withhold aid. We must learn to keep our emotions in check and remember the bigger picture. Making ourselves feel better is not the goal. Just "doing something" is not necessarily the best option. If we are truly interested in transformation, then we need to stop doing *for* people and start doing *with* people. That's much more difficult and will take a lot more time, but it's a shift that will be well worth the time and effort.

Build Capacity Rather Than Create Dependency

Two books by Daniel Rickett were immeasurably helpful as our church began to walk the path toward global partnership. *Building Strategic Relationships* and *Making Your Partnerships Work* ask and answer the very questions we were facing. In *Building Strategic Relationships,* Rickett tells a fictional story that demonstrates the difference between building capacity and creating dependency. The story is about a man who gives his friend a brand-new Mercedes Benz. At the conclusion of the story Rickett writes,

> The gift of the Mercedes Benz epitomizes what we all wish we could do for our brothers and sisters in the hard places of the world. If it is in our power to give what our brother or sister needs, we will happily give it for the sake of the gospel. But the story also triggers some disturbing questions.

> What makes me think my brother needs a Mercedes Benz? Do I know what he needs because he asked me? Or do I give a Mercedes because I think that's what he needs? Suppose my brother is making $20,000 a year. How is he going to afford the maintenance on a $60,000 Mercedes? My intention is to be generous, but my generosity becomes his burden.

> To have something to share is a wonderful thing. To give your brother what he needs when he needs it is even better. But because what is needed is not always apparent, giving can be a dangerous business.

> Those of us who partner with indigenous ministries face a subtle and constant danger. It's not primarily dependency, although that is the risk for which we are most often criticized. Nor is it paternalism, although we do slip into that more often than we care to admit. No, it is something harder to deal with than either of these. The most challenging question is this: *Have we contributed to the self-developing capabilities of our partners?* The surest way to prevent dependency is to pay close attention to *development*. It is also the best safeguard against paternalism. By focusing on development, we are forced to ask whether

our involvement makes our brothers and sisters better able to serve God according to their own gifts and calling. *Are we helping to build their capacity or are we simply relieving their needs?* (italics added)

Do you see the difference between *building capacity* and *creating dependency?* When we give something to someone in need, we have done one of those two things. Our gift can build their capacity, making them stronger, more stable, and healthier, with a greater potential for development and growth. On the other hand, our gift, though heartfelt and sincerely given, can invite them to become dependent on others for their growth, health and development. Our gift really can keep them stalled in a place of helplessness. We are either building their capacity or encouraging their dependency. That is a critical difference that will have a long-term impact one way or the other.

Unfortunately, there are plenty of global examples of gifts and projects that build unhealthy dependency. When we erect buildings, dig wells and start schools with foreign funding, plans, materials and labor, we haven't built the capacity of the national leaders. They don't feel a sense of ownership and healthy pride about those projects, and they're probably not going to repair or improve them. It's like giving a $60,000 Mercedes to someone who can't afford to maintain it. That's not a long-term solution. It's not doing *with* people. It's the wrong path to take.

Thankfully there is another option. There are projects and approaches that build the capacity of our global partners. Let me share my favorite example from our partnership in Kenya. About five years into our relationship, I was leading a team to serve in Karogoto. On the last day of the trip, we visited one of the eight villages that make up the community of Karogoto. As we approached the village, we couldn't help but notice a crowd of people lining the road. There were probably one hundred people hard at work, digging a three-foot trench that stretched about three hundred yards. After asking a few questions, we discovered that they were preparing to run pipes from the main water tank in the center of Karogoto to a distribution tank they had established in the center of their village of Kahiga. No one from the outside imposed this project on them. No one from the outside even suggested it. They saw the potential. They seized the opportunity. They were digging the trench. They were laying the pipe. And we were thrilled to discover that they had raised the money for it! Each family in this small, simple, rural village contributed whatever they could afford, so that they could have clean water in their own neighborhood. They saw no reason to wait for someone else to dig the trench, lay the pipe, or even supply the funding. They could do all that. And they did!

The primary well and water tank had been drilled and constructed a year earlier. Our church helped significantly with that project, but wasn't needed to help at all with this one. "Thanks! We can take it from here," was the prevailing attitude. Our contributions a year earlier had obviously built the capacity within the community. They were now better equipped to move forward on their own. That's a huge win!

Remember that if you're truly interested in development, *you don't measure your success by what you do for others. You measure your success by what they are now able to do for themselves.* That's why building capacity is a much better choice than creating dependency.

Empower Leaders Rather Than Address Needs

Kurt Kandler, Executive Director of The 410 Bridge (a global leader in Christ-centered, community initiated development and the organization that helps our church to partner with leaders in Kenya and Haiti), once told me that, "We're drawn to leaders, not needs. In fact, we're driven by leaders, not needs." The change in focus that he is describing – from needs to leaders – is a significant one. For some reason, most of us are quick to notice needs. We see how bad things are, how desperate the conditions, the crisis and the urgency. Those problems catch our eye. When we return from a trip, it's easy to show pictures and tell stories of the problems developing communities are facing. Trip participants aren't the only ones who tend to focus on the problems and challenges. Global nonprofits point our attention to the desperate needs and staggering shortages. Those images and stories create a sense of urgency, raise funds, and keep interest high. The needs are always in your face. The needs seem urgent. The needs scream for attention. And they are literally everywhere.

If you're drawn to, driven by, or focused on needs, you'll find yourself constantly pulled toward challenges that you will never overcome. Focusing on needs may tempt you to engage in all the wrong practices and set you up for failure. When you see nothing but the needs, you're far more likely to pursue short-term rather than long-term solutions. More often than not, you will start doing things *for* people rather than doing things *with* people. You'll engage in relief and build dependency, all in an effort to meet needs which, let's not forget, are endless. Starting with the needs sends you down a never-ending path with roadblocks that you simply cannot overcome.

Don't misunderstand where I'm going here. We cannot ignore the needs that people around the globe are facing. We're following Jesus, and He didn't ignore people's needs. As we saw in chapter five, He came to address all the needs that mankind is facing – the spiritual, physical and social needs. The way He did that was remarkable. Instead of focusing on the needs, He focused on leaders. He empowered leaders, and they literally changed the world. We're called to do the same.

When you seek to empower leaders rather than meet needs, you look for men and women of vision, character, and potential. You partner with the people that God has strategically placed in needy communities. God has prepared the way for leaders to lead their neighbors toward transformation. In other words, instead of looking at the needs, look for signs of God at work and for the people He is working through. Focusing on them isn't as urgent, but it is exponentially more important.

Not only will indigenous leaders be able to help you – by serving as "culture translators," explaining nuances and long-held traditions, keeping you from making awkward mistakes – but they are also the ones best positioned to help their own communities. When you mobilize, equip, and empower local leaders, they will create solutions to the current challenges and the obstacles that lie in the future. When you focus on *leaders*, you'll find the opportunity to build their capacity, working *with* them in an effort to bring about *long-term* change and community-wide transformation! This single shift – from looking for needs to locating leaders – makes all the difference. Make your goal to empower leaders rather than meet needs. You'll be glad you did.

Focused Rather Than Scattered

Scattered is easy. Lots of people are scattered, especially when it comes to global causes. It's trendy to "like" a movement, sign an e-petition, go to a film screening, wear a T-shirt or attend a concert. Soon, though, they're on to something else. A new word has been created to describe people with this tendency – slactivists. Slackers and activists rolled into one! They want to change the world, but they keep changing directions. This type of energy and passion is a great start. But it's far from the finish line. *What's desperately needed isn't a sprint, but a long walk in one direction.* When you do a lot of things, it's hard to do any of them really well. On the other hand, when you focus on just a few things, you have a good chance of making a deep impact. Focus is much more difficult but much more effective.

My friends, Duane and Daylin, pastor a church in Germany. On three occasions, my wife and I have been able to visit them there. One of the great things about visiting Europe is the inter-connectedness of all those little countries. You can hop on a train and get to another country in no time. Regardless of the city or country, some of Europe's most famous sites are the cathedrals. The architecture is amazing. The craftsmanship is unmatched. These cathedrals showcase an artistry and magnificent beauty that has lasted for centuries.

I can't imagine the time and effort that were required to craft those cathedrals, and the pain-staking attention given to minute details. Consider the fact that it took generations to see the project through to completion. These marvelous structures weren't built in a day, a year, or even a lifetime. The stonecutters and masons who worked on the initial phases of a cathedral were dead long before the church was completed. They never saw the finished product. To build something that would last for centuries, they had to invest at least decades. Building a cathedral wasn't a sprint; it was a long walk in one direction.

No one is building cathedrals anymore. Right down the road from my office, however, is a lot full of modular homes. Pre-fab. Assembly line. Crank 'em out one after another. That's how lots of construction is done these days. It's quicker, cheaper, easier and more efficient. That's fine when it comes to building projects. But, don't miss what it says about us as a society. We aren't as patient or as focused as previous generations were. We've gotten used to instant access and 4G results. We dash around doing a little bit of everything. Rarely do we channel our energy in one direction. When it comes to international partnerships and sustainable development, a scattered approach just won't work. We would be much more effective and provide much more help if we would focus our time, energy, and resources in one place (or a few places, depending on your size and scope) for a long time. Here are a few suggestions to help you or your church focus your global engagement:

- Rather than supporting dozens of ministries all over the globe, scale back and zero in on just a few. *Go a mile deep in just a few places rather than being spread an inch thin over many miles.*

- Don't expect a ten day trip to make a life-long difference in a community. Stop putting so much attention on what you're going to fix or build or accomplish in your brief visit. Don't stop going. Just stop sprinting.

- Go back to the same place year after year instead of globe-trotting all over the planet from one summer to the next. Returning to the same place speaks volumes about your commitment to those people in that place.

- Offer clear and consistent opportunities to people to engage in global outreach. They may not respond at first, but a repeated call will make a difference over time.

- Shift your attention from results to relationships, walking the long path of partnership together.

You'll be amazed at how much deeper you can go and how much more effective you can be when you're focused in one place or on one cause rather than being scattered all over map.

Partnership Essentials

If fish could talk, the one who was "saved" by the monkey would tell you that having good intentions is not the same as being intentional. Good intentions are a positive start, but not nearly enough to bring about long-term change. The five intentional actions outlined in this chapter allow us to do less harm and provide more help to our brothers and sisters around the world. Here they are once more: commit to the (1) *long-term rather than the short-term* by doing projects (2) *with people rather than for people.* This shift allows you to (3) *build capacity rather than create dependency* because you are (4) *empowering leaders rather than trying to meet needs.* All this is done in the context of a (5) *focused rather than scattered* strategy of global engagement. These intentional practices will take you down a path toward healthy global partnerships.

The first four chapters of this book answered the question, "*Why* should we pursue global engagement?" Chapters five through seven then unpacked *how* to develop healthy global partnerships. The next chapter will answer the question: "*Who* should we be partnering with?"

START WALKING
Notes and Next Steps

Walk This Way: How?

- Long-term rather than short-term.
- Do *with* rather than do *for*.
- Build capacity rather than create dependency.
- Empower leaders rather than meet needs.
- Focused rather than scattered.

Next Steps

- Duane Elmer's, *Cross-Cultural Servanthood* should be required reading for anyone serving cross-culturally.
- The three-part video series *Restore*, by LifeChurch.tv, is an invaluable training tool to help people get better at doing good. It can be found at www.youtube.com/user/LifeChurchtv.

8 WHAT A GREAT PARTNER LOOKS LIKE

We think we can partner with just about anyone.
On the contrary, a great partner fits a particular profile.

"There's someone I'd like you to meet. You two would be great together!"

By now, I hope you are convinced that the path of partnership is the way to go. You agree with the model. You're committed to the best practices. You're ready to walk this way. You just need one more thing before you can head down the path of partnership. You need a partner!

Forging global partnerships is new territory. It's not a well-worn trail. It is drastically different than sending a missionary to another country. Building a healthy cross-cultural partnership is not at all the same as hiring national leaders in an international community. Neither of those approaches – sending missionaries or hiring nationals – results in the kind of reciprocal connection that a partnership provides. *A true partnership is a mutually beneficial, two-way relationship in which both sides offer some of their strengths and resources, as well as receive some benefits and added value.* That's what we're looking to build. And, by definition, it's not something we can build on our own. We need to share a vision, lock arms, and move forward with another church, organization or people group. We need a partner for the path. But how do we find one? How do we know where to look or even what to look for?

When our church started down this path, we tripped and stumbled. We learned some lessons and tried again. We got turned around a bit and meandered for a while. But we kept growing and learning and walking. We're still not skipping along perfectly, but we're doing better than we were before. We've figured out what to avoid and what to pursue in a potential partner. In fact, in the process of looking for that perfect someone, we actually got to know a partner who would be perfect for you. I'm serious! If you've embraced the vision of global partnership and are simply looking for someone to walk the path with you, then look no further. Allow me to introduce you to Partnership Pablo.

Hola, Pablo!

Meet my good friend, Pablo. He enjoys sunsets, ethnic foods, and long walks on dirt trails. Each part of him represents an essential quality of a great global partner.

Head: Indigenous
Hands: Reciprocal and Relational
Body: Compatible
Legs: Independent

Independent: Standing on His Own Two Feet

A great partner has established independence and is standing on his own two feet. He is walking a bold path, moving toward a homegrown vision, employing and/or empowering national leaders, and making his own decisions based on the local conditions. He is not being driven by outsiders like foreign donors, U.S. churches, western boards, or even well-meaning missionaries. A potential partner has moved from dependence to independence. Great partners are ready to move with you from independence to interdependence. Consider the following continuum:

Dependent - - - - - - Independent - - - - - - Interdependent

Everyone and every organization begins on the left side. We were all helplessly dependent at some point. Infants are dependent on their mothers. Start-ups are dependent on their venture capital. Church-plants are dependent on their sending church or organization or perhaps just the "tent-making" income that the leadership relies on in the early days. No healthy person or group wants to stay in this stage. Over time, with growth and maturity, people and organizations develop strength and independence. Children begin a journey of figuring out how to care for themselves. Start-ups get to the point where they are generating enough revenue to cover their expenses and consider some expansion. Churches move toward self-sufficiency, supporting their own leaders and funding their own programs. This is independence.

Of course, there are still set-backs, and there may even be challenging seasons when they are forced to become dependent again (seeking a bail-out, taking out a loan, moving back home into Dad and Mom's basement, etc.). But hopefully, there are growing levels of strength and autonomy. There is movement from dependence to independence. Only then are individuals and groups able to continue toward interdependence. At that point, they begin leaning on and drawing from others, not so they can survive (as when they were dependent), but so they can thrive.

Only someone who is independent has the margin, the resources, and the potential to give from his excess to strengthen and mobilize others. Churches, organizations or groups that have attained this level of independence are potential partners. The best prospects are ones who have moved from dependence to independence and are now ready to explore a relationship of interdependence.

Unfortunately, well-meaning U.S. churches and individuals sabotage the process toward independence time and time again. Rather than helping global pastors and national churches to struggle through the growing pains between dependence and independence, donors step in and hire or support nationals to continue the work they are doing in their native community. It is such an appealing option that well-intentioned Westerners rarely see the damage it causes. It seems like we are clearing the path and paving the way for effective ministry. "If we could just subsidize their income," we tell ourselves, "they could be free to focus on ministry. And thanks to a great international exchange rate, the cost to us is so small. How could we not offer this national pastor our support? Now he can quit his other job and focus all his energy on the ministry."

This scenario is not at all uncommon. The traditional missions model attracts lots of international Christian leaders. Many come to the U.S. hoping that we will support and send them back to their communities. Lots of churches are intrigued by that option, and entire agencies have been built on the model of hiring nationals. It's promoted as a great global opportunity with "lots of bang for your buck!" The trouble is, this path is not healthy, not sustainable and not reproducible. The national leader will stop earning a local income and instead rely on funding from abroad. That's not sustainable. His church may see that he's now taken care of and stop giving sacrificially to support him. That's not healthy. Furthermore, after watching this process unfold, young, potential pastors and leaders conclude that the path to ministry isn't a local path, but rather one that must detour through the U.S. in search of donors. That's not reproducible. Consequently, rather than helping these global leaders forge a truly independent and indigenous movement, we invite them to become dependent on us, making it impossible for them to move toward the other two stages of maturity. The path we've created is literally moving them in the wrong direction and keeping them in unhealthy dependence, rather than encouraging healthy (albeit challenging) independence.

I have no doubt that the stated goal is to eventually transition to independence. If that's the case, then why build such elaborate dependence on foreign funding? Why not begin with the value of independence and figure out how to make that part of the DNA? *Do the hard work early. Build independence into the fabric from the very beginning and look for potential partners who have done the same.* A great partner is one who is independent, standing on his own two feet and looking for an opportunity to walk with you towards interdependence.

Compatible: *What's at the Core?*

Moving to the next quality of our friend Pablo, we come to the torso – the body and core that forms the center of our global brother. This area represents the heart, the beliefs, and the motivation of a potential partner. At the center, there must be compatibility between partners. Specifically, we're looking for shared doctrinal beliefs and basic theological alignment. Here's the key though: we're looking for shared belief and alignment around the core issues of our faith, not personal preferences.

None of us holds all our beliefs with the same degree of certainty. Nor are all of our beliefs essential to our faith. Certainly some are non-negotiable, comprising the epicenter of the Christian faith. You would die for these beliefs because to deny them would be to deny something critical and essential. It's these beliefs that set someone apart as a follower of Jesus. People who share these beliefs with us will also share God's Kingdom with us.

Yet not all our beliefs belong in that center ring. We all have beliefs that we hold with less certainty. Whether we like to admit it or not, these beliefs are not essential to the Christian faith. Hopefully, you can think of some of your beliefs that would fall into this category. For me, it's theories about the End Times or modes of baptism or the outworking of the Holy Spirit. I know what I believe about these issues, but I don't hold them to be an essential part of the Christian faith. I wouldn't die for these specific beliefs. Maybe you would. In that case, I bet you have other beliefs that you hold with less certainty. Surely you can admit that some of your theological beliefs are not essential. If that's the case, then you probably shouldn't spend too much time separating over those issues. Men and women of God – true followers of Jesus – differ on many non-essential beliefs, sometimes significantly. Their differences, however, don't exclude them from the family of God. If they are

WHAT A GREAT PARTNER LOOKS LIKE

included in the family of God, why would we not include them in partnership at some level?

You'll do well to gain clarity about the levels of your beliefs. Ask yourself which of your beliefs are core and which are peripheral. Identifying what's at the center allows us to focus on the beliefs that are most important. It also reminds us that our distinctives shouldn't divide us. That opens up so many opportunities and introduces so much freedom. Knowing what's at the core will give you clarity as you pursue global partners. Incidentally, gaining clarity about what's at the core will not only help you identify potential global partners, but will also introduce you to opportunities in your local context. You may discover churches and ministries in your region who have differing distinctive beliefs, but who share your core beliefs. Believe it or not, those folks are teammates! Imagine the impact that local or regional ministry partnerships could have. It's amazing what happens when we focus on how much we have in common with our brothers and sisters, rather than the peripheral issues that divide us. The connections and possibilities abound.

Consider what happened in Karogoto, Kenya, when the local pastors began to recognize who their teammates are. Like many Kenyan villages, Karogoto has a "village center." It may not be the geographic center, but it's a place clearly understood to be the heart of the community. Here you'll find the shops, main road, gathering places and churches. Deliverance Church is on one end of the square. God's Grace and Glory (G3) is on the other end. Just down the road from G3 is the Lord's Vineyard. Across the road from Deliverance is Antioch Baptist. No matter which church you attend, you're coming to the same part of the village on Sunday!

Sadly, there was a time not long ago when, even though they shared such physical proximity, these churches had almost no interaction with each other. Even worse, their leaders and congregants had negative interactions with each other. They chose to emphasize what made them different from one another, failing to see the common core that bound them together. Thankfully, that's no longer the case.

Inspired by the leadership of Pastor Harrison Wabiru, five of the pastors of Karogoto now serve on the community's leadership council! Drawn together by a vision for unity and transformation in their community, they focus less on the needs of their particular churches and more on the opportunities in the community-at-large. Consequently, they've shifted their attention from the distinctive beliefs that make them unique to the core creed that binds them together. Each is a genuine follower of Jesus, and each is playing his part in the Body as Christ builds His church. Suspicion and competition have been replaced by trust and brotherhood. It's a beautiful picture of partnership. And here's a literal picture of the partnership:

From left to right, we have Pastor Robert (Agape Church),
Pastor James (Deliverance Church), Pastor David (The Lord's Vineyard),
Pastor Stephen (God's Grace and Glory), and myself. Pastor David from
Antioch Baptist Church couldn't be with us that day.

WHAT A GREAT PARTNER LOOKS LIKE

Motivated by their partnership with each other, our church has
come alongside this leadership council. They've demonstrated that
they are compatible with one another, and, in the process, invited
us to share in that compatibility. As we initially interacted with
them, we recognized that there is alignment around the core issues
of faith. We also realized that, by coming alongside them, we could
be part of the transformation they were moving toward. My hope
is that now we can bring that same mindset of compatibility that
we've discovered in a global setting to our local context. What if,
not just overseas but here at home, we were bound together with
those who share a core creed, rather than divided from those with
doctrinal distinctives? Just think of the statement that would make
to the watching world.

Compatibility is an essential part of the partnership profile. Be sure
that there is agreement at the core. When you discover
compatibility with independent believers, then you're on the path
toward partnership. You're not quite there yet though. There are
three more elements to look for in a partner.

Indigenous: The Face of the Place

Your global partners need to be indigenous. You're looking to
come alongside the *national leaders* in a particular global community.
Your partners need to be "the face of the place." Certainly
outsiders (like us) have a role to play, but that role must be
secondary to the role that the indigenous people of God play in
their communities.

We've already spent plenty of time on this theme. God is at work
not just here, but everywhere. Surely, the LORD is in this place. He
is omnipresent and that presence is offering grace and moving
toward redemption. God was present and at work long before the
first outsiders entered the picture. So when we, as outsiders, enter a
new context we want to identify and join the work of God among

the indigenous leaders within that particular context.

There are far too many examples of outsiders forging ahead without the wisdom of national leaders. Think of the church buildings that litter the African continent, buildings designed, built and funded by American's under the oversight of an American missionary. Picture the hospital in South America that's directed and staffed by North Americans who receive their funding, direction and shipments of medical supplies from abroad. Consider the elementary school in Asia that gets its curriculum from the West and is powered by a revolving cycle of teachers serving one-year commitments. These churches, hospitals and schools are not indigenous movements. The "faces" of these places are foreign.

I'm not being critical of the people, the passion or the impact represented in these examples. The sacrifice, commitment and dedication necessary to pioneer works like these is beyond what I could offer. I honor the commitment and respect the people who develop these kinds of works. However, because these projects are not built on indigenous leadership they don't represent the kinds of things that we are looking to partner with. At their foundation, they are fundamentally different than something built by national leaders.

When you look for partners, you must look for indigenous leaders who are developing a plan that fits within their context and is built with their resources. *Partner with someone who is authentic to that community and doing something that is indigenously sustainable and reproducible.*

Finding and nurturing something like that will take *a lot* more time. But it will have *a lot* more potential for bringing lasting change to the community. Indigenous leadership is the key to lasting transformation. That's why it's one of the primary things for you to look for in a global partner.

Reciprocal: Give and Receive

The last two qualities in a global partner are closely related. They
are Partnership Pablo's two arms. One is reciprocity; the other is
relationship. Let's talk about reciprocity first. This is what the
Apostle Paul was referring to when he wrote to the Romans with
the hope of being "mutually encouraged by each other's faith
(Romans 1:12)." Like him, you should look to develop partnerships
that are reciprocal, avoiding arrangements where the resources are
only flowing in one direction. Instead, you want a back-and-forth,
give-and-take, two-way flowing relationship.

This doesn't mean that both partners are offering the same thing to
the relationship. That wouldn't be much of a partnership. If both
partners had the same resources, insights, strengths and gifts to
offer, then there would be no value in joining together. Healthy
partners don't offer the same things to the relationship, but they do
both offer something. Each partner needs to be aware of what he
has to offer and be willing to offer it. This may not be intuitive, and
it will probably take some time and conversation to figure out.
Consequently, *both potential partners need to at least embrace the value of
reciprocity*. They need to be on the same page about this concept.
Early in the relationship, they may not know what they have to
offer or what they need to receive. That's okay and understandable.
They should, however, be open to the idea of establishing a give-
and-take, reciprocal arrangement. In the course of conversation
and prayer over a period of time, both partners will begin to
identify resources they have that could benefit the partnership. If
they've already embraced the value of reciprocity, then they will be
poised to act accordingly. Like parts of a healthy body, both
partners can offer something out of their excess that will contribute
to something that the other partner is lacking.

A few examples may be helpful. Typically, we in the West are able
to offer optimism, hope, creativity, and ingenuity. On the other

hand, we have so much to learn from our brothers and sisters around the world when it comes to living in community, walking by faith, offering compassion, and trusting in God's provision. As we share with each other, hear from each other, and pray for each other, our respective strengths spill over and begin to rub off on each other.

Perhaps a more tangible example is also in order. A few years ago, we collaborated with our partners in Haiti to provide a water solution for their community. Both partners (the leaders at our church and the leaders in Maliarette) had to bring something unique to the table in order to see any forward movement. Our Haitian partners had to drive the process. They needed to offer leadership and direction. This was their community and their problem. They had to develop their own solution since they knew better than us what type of water system would bring long-term benefit and sustainable development. They had to do the hard work of research, exploration, planning and budgeting. The project couldn't move forward until they proposed a detailed action plan that moved us toward a solution.

Ironically, participants from the West often want to offer a plan of action as their contribution to the partnership. We typically feel qualified to provide solutions and propose plans. Granted, our proposals may be helpful at times, but they are rarely the best things for us to offer to the partnership. It is much better for our national partners to offer the plans and proposals. The globe is smattered with examples of "solutions" that well-meaning Westerners developed, funded and implemented. The vast majority of these have failed to bring long-term, sustainable development.

So when it came to developing a solution for their water problems, our national partners in Haiti led the way. They analyzed the current realities, took stock of their assets and proposed a way forward. In the process, they recognized their need for support from outsiders. As is often the case in developing communities, the local people could offer a portion but not all of the financial capital needed to complete the project. Furthermore, since they were working against inertia and perhaps generations of inactivity, our Haitian brothers and sisters needed help building momentum and excitement. We quickly realized that those were contributions our church could offer! We could raise funds, inject excitement and kick-start the project. We began with a campaign called H2O4H (water for Haiti), which generated enough money to launch phase one of a water solution. Then, by sending short-term teams to serve alongside our partners, we were able to provide excitement in the community, creating momentum and mobilizing the members of the village to take action and continue down this path, a path that has led to clean water for the entire community!

Each partner brought a unique contribution. Both of us offered something tangible and critical to the solution. This kind of reciprocity is a beautiful thing. If you are looking for a partner, make sure before you proceed that the national leaders you are interacting with are committed to pursuing reciprocity.

Relational: In This Together

This arm is similar to the other. The first points to reciprocity; this one to relationship. As we explored in chapter six, life is about relationships: God's relationship with people, their relationships with each other and our relationship with the rest of creation. Relationships are what is broken in this world, and they are what must be restored. All this to say, relationships are central to healthy global engagement. Healing *relationships* is paramount.

You need to keep that emphasis in the front of your mind as you consider possible global partners. Obviously on the front end of interactions, there is no way to know how deep and wide a relationship will become. However, you need to at least make sure that both sides are committed to building a relationship. That must be a high value, and there must be practices in place that allow you to live out this value.

When our church was looking for a partner in South Africa, we visited and interacted with several national leaders – pastors, educators and social workers. One in particular stood out because of the breadth of his work in response to the HIV/AIDS epidemic. His organization had established care facilities, micro-businesses, hospice units and more. Needless to say, our team was impressed, so we started to evaluate this organization according to our partnership profile. They seemed to be operating independently, perhaps even interdependently. Their core doctrine looked to be compatible with ours. They were certainly indigenously led. I could see the potential for reciprocity in that they knew what they could provide and what they wanted us to provide. However, what they wanted us to provide let me know that they were not really interested in a relationship. Simply put, the contribution they were looking for from us was financial. Period. They simply needed more funds so they could continue to expand their work. I didn't get the sense that they had the time, energy or desire for another relationship. They weren't really looking to get to know and grow with us. Rather, they were inviting us to invest in what they were doing. That's not necessarily a bad thing. In many circumstances that would be quite appropriate. But it wasn't what we were looking for. We were looking for a relational partnership. They were looking for financial donors. I'm not sure we would have noticed that distinction had we not been intentional about including *relationships* in our partnership profile. We're looking for partners who are committed to relationships.

Let me quickly clarify one thing before moving on from this point. Don't be too quick to rule out a potential partner just because they don't provide the kinds of relationships you'd like. Often times, when we think of global relationships, we think of personal interactions between U.S. believers and national believers around the world. In some situations, those are possible and valuable. In other scenarios, those kinds of relationships are not best. In fact, they may actually hinder some partnerships and endanger some partners.

Our friends at She is Safe (SIS) helped us understand this. SIS works to prevent, rescue, and restore women and girls from abuse and exploitation in high-risk places around the world. They are deeply committed to relationships, especially the redemptive ones that their indigenous teammates are building in the countries in which they serve. U.S. teams often want to visit these locations, but that's typically not helpful and often unwise. And even though SIS is committed to relationships, they are not willing to compromise their work around the world or jeopardize the safety of their partners in order to provide American mission teams a short-term global experience. As a result, your church may not have the chance to make the relational connections you may have had in mind. That doesn't mean SIS isn't committed to relationships. On the contrary, it is their commitment to indigenous, redemptive relationship that drives their decisions and makes them such an effective partner. Simply put, great international partners are committed to relationships: redemptive relationships in the countries in which they serve, and healthy relationships with global partners.

What if There is No Pablo?

Partnership Pablo provides a great checklist of qualities to look for in potential partners. But what if there is no Pablo? What if there is no local church or Christian movement? In a world with so many unreached people groups, how do we build ministry partnerships in the places of greatest need?

These are good questions, and they often come up in conversations about global partnership. So it seems fitting to say a few words on this topic. Let me begin by saying that I am by no means an expert on reaching the unreached and engaging the unengaged. Others are much more qualified to help us figure out the best strategies and approaches. That being said, here are a few thoughts about building partnership in a world that still has so many people who are unreached and unengaged with Jesus:

- God is still at work, not just here and there, but everywhere, even in places that seem unreached. There may not be a strong local church, an established training school, or a translation of the Bible into the local dialect, but make no mistake, God is still present and active. Begin with that conviction. Look for evidence to support it. Discover where and how He is working and join Him.

- Western missionaries are probably not going to be openly accepted and well-received in many of these places. Because of our history, our tendency to overestimate our role, and the huge cultural gap between the U.S. and most unreached people groups, we may not be the best ones to pioneer a redemptive work. It seems like "near neighbors" will have much easier access and are more strategically placed to make in-roads into unreached people groups. Our brothers and sisters in sub-Saharan Africa have great access to northern Africa's unreached regions. The believers in Asia have an open door into "closed countries" in the Middle East. Even South American Christ-followers have more opportunities to enter limited-access countries than North Americans have. In other words, just because places may be "closed" to U.S. missionaries doesn't mean they are "closed" to everyone.

- Healthy global partnerships would still provide a great path. Our partnership with near neighbors could be the very best way to join what God is doing in the unreached and unengaged parts of the world.

I've heard of North American churches partnering with our brothers and sisters in South America to send Latinos to unreached people groups in the Middle East. That seems like a fantastic idea. I'm personally familiar with a similar opportunity growing out of a college in South Africa. Cornerstone Institute is a dynamic Christian liberal arts college that is training students from over a dozen African and Middle Eastern countries. These students are graduating as pastors, counselors, teachers, and business leaders. Many come from countries with unreached people groups and are returning to those very countries after graduation, poised to reach and lead their own people. That seems like a wise and effective way to join what God is doing in those hard to reach places.

If we are willing to partner with God's people in strategic places, the opportunities to reach the unreached and unengaged are greater than ever. Dan Rickett, a true expert in this matter, has a great perspective on this:

> You can find communities of Christian witness nearly everywhere. And they are growing. Few places remain where North Americans should pioneer a ministry without at least conferring with local Christians and others who are also active in the area.

> I certainly am not suggesting that world evangelization is coming to a close or that there is no place for North American missionaries. On the contrary, the task has never been larger or the cost greater than it is today. Billions of people do not know Jesus Christ as Savior and Lord. Many of them live in nations where Christians are harassed, imprisoned, or even executed because of their faith. Yet in spite of the cost, local Christians are sharing the love of Christ and planting churches with astonishing success, very often in places out of reach to conventional missionary methods. Their courage and sacrifice calls for our

partnership, but not necessarily our technology, our methodology, or our wealth. What it calls for, and what Majority World Christians ask for, is our personal, passionate involvement as co-workers in the ministry of the gospel."

Even in a world with so many unreached and unengaged, the path of partnership is still the best path to move down. We'd do well to lock arms with brothers and sisters who are independent, compatible, indigenous, reciprocal and relational. Global alliances with partners like that will enable us to reach the unreached and engage the unengaged.

Mucho Gusto, Pablo!

That's Pablo! He's a great global partner. He's standing on his own two feet of *independence*. At his core there's *compatibility* with who you are at your center. The face of the partnership is *indigenous*, showing the color and the culture of his national context. And he's reaching out with arms that are *relational* and *reciprocal*. That's who you're looking to partner with!

Now that we know why, how, and with whom we are partnering, let's turn our attention to *what* we can do to move down the path of global partnership.

START WALKING
Notes and Next Steps

Walk This Way: With Whom?

Look for a partner who is . . .

- independent
- compatible
- indigenous
- reciprocal
- relational

Next Steps

- To meet and interact with Partnership Pablo, visit **www.WalkThisWay.world**.
- A few organizations that could help you build healthy global partnerships include the **410 Bridge**, the **Global Hope Network** and the **Slavic Gospel Association**.

9 THREE STEPS TO GET YOU STARTED

You may feel like you can't do much to engage in global ministry. But, in fact, there are three simple steps you can take right now.

We live in a broken world. Spiritually, we are separated from God, billions having never heard of the rescue that He offers. Socially, we are estranged from and at odds with each other. Some, perhaps more than at any other time in human history, feel the full weight of that relational brokenness as they are bought and sold as slaves. Physically, all of us feel the effects of sickness, disease, hunger, and thirst. Children are the most vulnerable among us, and consequently, far too many children on the planet live in poverty or poor health. If our world were defined only by the brokenness, it would be a grim and hopeless place to call home.

But God is present here. He is not absent; in fact, He is active. He is on the move at all times and in every place. He is proactively bringing hope and offering restoration to every person on every square inch of the globe. No matter where you point your compass or set your sights, you could hang the banner, *"Surely the LORD is in this place."* Since He is here, we have hope.

Since God is here, we have an opportunity to be part of something great. He has prepared the way for us, and now He invites us to walk with Him down the path of partnership. He calls us to lock arms with a diverse and beautiful collection of His children, doing His work and spreading His fame around the world. He calls us to go where He is leading and join what He is doing, to play our part in His global Body and get involved in the global transformation He is orchestrating. He invites us to *walk this way*.

Here are three steps you can take to start down that path: pray specifically, give wisely, and go where you are invited.

Pray Specifically

The first step is one you can take immediately, and it's probably the best step you can take toward global engagement. That is to pray specifically. Through prayer, we can instantly and constantly join what God is doing around the world. Prayer somehow moves God's hand while also molding our hearts. Prayer re-centers us on who God is and reminds us that He is at work, not just here but everywhere. Prayer takes us beyond our efforts and taps us into God's power, underlining the fact that transformation is not something we can do but something that only God can do. Prayer brings us back to the fact that at the heart, global partnerships are about relationships – relationships with brothers and sisters around the world, men, women and children who we are connected to us through Jesus. Prayer strengthens those connections just as much, if not more, than our physical activity or financial investment. And let's not forget, prayer is something that anyone can do. No matter who you are or where you are, you can be part of the global story God is writing when you pray.

Don't simply pray, though. Pray *specifically*. Consider Mark Batterson's challenge in *The Circle Maker*. He writes:

> A few years ago, I read one sentence that changed the way
> I pray. The author, pastor of one of the largest churches in

Seoul, Korea, wrote, "God does not answer vague prayers." When I read that statement, I was immediately convicted by how vague my prayers were. Some of them were so vague that there was no way of knowing whether God had answered them or not.

Praying specifically will require some effort, but the work will be worthwhile. You'll need to learn a bit about what God is doing around the world before you can pray specifically about it. That research will take some work, but the data is at your fingertips and the effort will be rewarded. Previous generations simply didn't have this opportunity. Amazingly, you can learn about God's movement in just about any place on the planet. Take advantage of this access. If you need a place to start, look no further than *Operation World*. It is a country-by-country guide that provides a great glimpse of what God is doing not just here, but everywhere.

You may not even need to find or research a global location. You may already have some international connections that you just haven't thought too much about. Does your church serve with people around the globe? Do you support or know of missionaries in a particular location? Do you have family ties or relational connections to cross-cultural communities? Take some time to think about the international connections you already have. Then ask God if He wants you to deepen any of these connections through specific prayer.

Once you have a country, region or people group in mind, learn as much as you can about what God is doing there. Ask questions like: *What's going well? Where are the signs of God's presence and movement? What are the challenges? Where are the obstacles and roadblocks?* Stay connected to that stream of information and then make that a stream of intentional prayer. Don't lazily ask God to "be with them." Hopefully by now you're fully convinced that He is already with them. Since that's the case, pray specifically about what you want the God of the universe to do in and through His global children. Pray for the pastors and leaders who are mobilizing their churches and communities toward transformation. Ask God to grant them wisdom, courage, and love for their people. Pray for the indigenous leaders, that they would find favor and build trust in their communities. Pray for the schools, teachers, and administrators who are shaping the next generation. Pray specifically.

When our church begins to interact with a potential partner, the first thing I talk to those national leaders about is how we can pray for each other. Before any money is donated, before teams start coming and going, before projects are planned, funded and underway, I want to know what's happening and what I can be praying about. Those signs of God at work – updates from the local churches, challenges in the community, personal needs and details, etc. – those are the things that we as a church begin to talk about and pray about. Few things are more exciting than seeing God answer these types of global prayers. He's done that several times. Let me share two examples from Kenya.

On my very first visit to Karogoto, our team gathered with a group of community leaders in one of the village's churches. That's where we first met Karogoto's leaders and heard their vision for their community. Sitting on wooden benches, our feet kicking up red dust, we prayed specifically for God to do something great by bringing transformation to this community. We didn't know it at the time, but those prayers would be the first step in a great partnership. Not long after that first meeting, the building in which we met was vacated. The congregation that had been meeting there outgrew the facility and moved to a larger one. Some time later, the property where the vacant church stood was purchased by the community's council. Service teams from our church found themselves on that very piece of land several times over the next few years. One team helped to demolish the worn-out building, clearing the land and making it ready for a new construction. The next team helped with the new construction, and another team was actually present as the finishing touches were put on a brand-new building – a facility that would house the knitting business and, hopefully one day, a medical clinic. All that transformation, development and progress took place on the very spot where we first met and prayed specifically with our partners!

A second story of answered prayer is starting to unfold in Karogoto. Each time a team visits, one of the highlights is a hike up a nearby hill. The entire community of Karogoto stretches out beneath it, so it's a great place to get a bird's-eye view of the village. The top of the hill is more than scenic though. To the pastors in Karogoto, it is sacred. Each one of them received their call to ministry on that hill. Many, perhaps all, of them have spent days and nights fasting and praying on that hill. Technically, it's just a hill. To our ministry partners, it is holy ground. So many prayers have been offered from atop and answered within its shadow. So it is only fitting that each visiting team spends some time in prayer on that hill.

As only God can, He is answering those prayers in remarkable ways. All those prayers by all those pastors and all those teams have been raised just outside Karogoto, in a neighboring community called Tumutumu. And, even though many of those prayers may not have been spoken specifically for Tumutumu, they are being answered specifically in Tumutumu! Over the past months, the leaders in Karogoto have felt a burden to share some of what they have learned and received with these neighbors. A leadership council has been formed. A vision has been embraced. The people of Tumutumu are beginning to work together and move forward toward community development. In just one year, a water system was proposed, funded and implemented. Clean, fresh drinking water now flows to the Tumutumu Primary School, not far from the base of the hill where so many prayers have been lifted!

Praying specifically is a great first step in global engagement. Stay informed about what's going on. Talk to God about what He's doing and how you can join Him as he brings transformation to a community. Don't underestimate what can happen when you start to pray specifically for a global community and its leaders.

Give Wisely

As you're informed and in prayer about God's work in a particular place, you may soon discover ways you can join His work in that place. You may very well have resources that could dramatically accelerate the development, life-change and transformation that God is orchestrating. Chances are, there will be projects that need funding. Giving towards these projects may be a step that God wants you to take. If so, take that step. Don't stay on the bench when God wants you in the game. Don't put it off or make excuses. *Find ways to free up funds so they can be channeled toward the global transformation that God is orchestrating.* You'd be shocked at the impact that a seemingly small gift can make when it's given wisely towards global development.

Keep in mind though that not all giving is wise. Some has very little impact or, as we've seen in previous chapters, may even have a negative impact. That shouldn't stop you from giving altogether; it should simply stop you from giving without first learning as much as you can about the actual impact of your giving. Notice that "Give Wisely" follows "Pray Specifically." Before you give, seek wisdom from God and from wise leaders. Don't let the emotions of a heart-breaking moment override the wisdom of healthy engagement.

I can't possibly say all that needs to be said on this topic. Whole books have been written on this subject alone. One of the best is Jonathan Martin's appropriately titled *Giving Wisely?* A key learning from Martin's experience is that we need to allow our giving to be

116

guided by trusted relationships with indigenous leaders. Without those relationships, it's risky, even foolish, to give toward the things that you perceive to be needs. Meeting physical needs is not going to bring transformation; relationships are. So, if our giving is growing out of positive relationships and furthering those relationships, then it has the power to do a lot of good. Simply put, we give wisely when we follow the guidance of a wise and trusted partner. If the relationship is strong, your partners will let you know what gifts would be most healthy, helpful, and sustainable.

In my experience, I have found that healthy relationships with global partners have led to two kinds of giving opportunities: on-going sponsorships and one-time projects.

On-Going Sponsorships

I love the life-on-life connection that child sponsorship offers. In fact, right now as I'm writing this, my son Jackson, who is eight years old, is upstairs writing to Lameck, a ten-year old Kenyan student who our family sponsors. Not long ago, Jackson was able to join me on a trip to Karogoto, where Lameck lives. That's when I took this heart-warming shot of the two of them:

We arrived on Saturday. On Sunday evening, as Jack and I were getting ready for bed, he said to me, "Dad, it's so weird. Lameck and I just met yesterday, and we're already best friends!" That kind of connection and global vision is well worth the monthly sponsorship payment. And that doesn't even touch on the benefits that Lameck, his family, his school and his community are receiving from our small on-going contribution.

Most of us can find a way to free about $40 a month to invest in life-change. That is indeed what takes place through a good sponsorship program. The sponsored students receive spiritual, academic, medical and physical support. Families of sponsored students find their burden easier to bear and their hope strengthened. Churches and schools in sponsorship communities receive resources and momentum. Sponsorship funds truly have an exponential impact.

The cover story of the June 2013 edition of *Christianity Today* explored child sponsorship and the life-changing impact it's having. The title of the article provides a fitting summary: "Want to Change the World? Sponsor a Child." I whole-heartedly agree with the findings. I've seen the impact first-hand. I am so glad that organizations like The 410 Bridge, Compassion International and World Vision are facilitating excellent child sponsorship programs. They're committed to healthy development and many, if not all, of the best practices we've explored. Sponsoring a child through a trusted organization like one of these is a great way for you to give wisely toward global transformation.

Student sponsorship has been a great on-ramp into global engagement for hundreds of people in our church. A relatively small percentage of people at our church will actually go on a short-term trip, but a much larger percentage can engage in global transformation through sponsorship. Not only do they give, but they also pray for and correspond with the students they sponsor.

They are building relationships that lead to transformation. It's been a great way to get lots of people involved in global development. Student sponsorship is one way to give wisely. Projects are another.

One-Time Projects

Contributing toward community-initiated development projects creates momentum and is often a catalyst for transformation in a community. Joining your partners as they implement water systems, micro-businesses and building construction may be a great way for you to start giving. It's worth mentioning again that these projects need to be community-initiated, healthy, and sustainable. *Unhealthy giving does more harm than good, so give wisely – and then give generously.* Give within the context of a relationship toward projects that will build capacity. That kind of giving gets you off the sidelines and into the action, making you a stakeholder in the transformation that is underway.

Three times in the last year, our church raised funds for a project initiated by our partners in Maliarette, Haiti. We were shocked when we learned that a staggering 80% of the children in Haiti have no access to formal education. Our shock shifted to engagement when we learned that our Haitian partners did something to change that statistic, at least in Maliarette. They started the first-ever school in that community. Refusing to underestimate their role and using whatever gifts they had, they recruited teachers, engaged families, and gathered students under a tree for daily lessons. On rainy days, they set up a tarp! Before long, they had two administrators, four teachers, and seventy-five students going to school every day!

Wanting to support our partners and encourage the steps they were taking, we raised funds for a school building (designed, developed, and proposed by the Haitian leaders in Maliarette). During a 30Hour Fast held by our student ministries early in the year, middle school and high school students at our church raised nearly $30,000 for the project. Later in the year, adults, eager to pour on their contributions, added more than $17,000 for the school.

My favorite donations came on the first Sunday of a campaign we called "Pour it On." After church, I was having dinner with my family, explaining what dad and mom did in "big church" while my four kids talked about what happened in their areas. I told them about students, just like them, who were having school under a tree. I shared what our partners in Haiti were doing about this and how our church could join that movement by investing in a school building project. Without missing a beat, Jackson shot up from the table and ran to his room. When he returned, he had two five-dollar bills in hand. One was his and one belonged to his younger sister, Andie. (He assumed Andie would be as eager and generous as he was. Thankfully, he was right!) They saw a need, recognized what they could do to help, and wisely decided to give!

Those two campaigns – the student's 30Hour Fast and the summer's "Pour it On" program – provided enough capital to complete four classrooms and the restrooms. To finish out the year, we offered our church one more opportunity to give toward the school in Haiti. Our Christmas goal was to raise $18,500 to construct one more classroom, this one for the third-graders in Maliarette. Throughout the month of December, nearly $21,000 poured in for the third-graders!

One donation envelope contained a stack of checks and this note from a trio of triplets who attend our church:

> *Our names are Jena, Jade and Joey and we love going to Epic Kidz.*
> *We are in the third grade in the Scranton School District. Recently*
> *our Mom and Dad told us how our church is raising money to build*
> *a third grade classroom in Maliarette, Haiti. Our parents also told*
> *us how the children meet outside under a tent for school. Being in the*

third grade this made us all realize how lucky we are. We are thankful for all the nice things we have and realize that these children need help.

We recently turned 9. All of us agreed that instead of getting presents and toys for our birthday we would ask our family and friends to donate money to the Pour it On campaign at church. We are so happy to say that we raised $500 for these children! Please accept this donation, as we really want to help out with the new classroom!

- Jena, Jade, Joey

Throughout the year, it was amazing to watch young and old alike give whatever they could give to this life-changing partnership project.

You can do that too. You can find creative ways to generate income or free up funds. You can find a sponsorship opportunity or a project that grows out of a trusted relationship. You can join what God is doing. You can be a stakeholder in the transformation. All you have to do is give wisely. Step one: *pray specifically*. Step two: *give wisely*. Step three: *go where you are invited*.

Go Where You Are Invited

Your relationship with your brothers and sisters around the world may open the door for you to go and physically join them in the work that God is doing in their neighborhood. You shouldn't demand this though. As we've already explored, some partnerships and some parts of the world are not conducive to hosting teams of visitors. Going isn't always a good idea. In some places, we'd be in the way. In others, we would put our brothers' and sisters' lives at risk. Some times you should go; some times you shouldn't. Here's the key: *only go where you are invited*. If you are invited, and if God is affirming that invitation, then you should get up and go!

In many cases, you should go simply to be with your partners around the world. Physically showing up and being present with them speaks volumes about your commitment to the relationship and your belief in them and their community. Don't keep your distance, simply writing checks from afar. Go. Visit. Be with your partners. Stay connected and invested and ready to show up from time-to-time, tangibly reminding your global partners that they are not alone, but rather connected to the global Body of Christ.

As well as being an unmistakable reminder of your relationship, your visits may go even further in their impact. You may be able to provide resources, expertise, training or perspective that is desperately needed. You may be able to supply for your partners something that they are lacking that you have in abundance. You only discover that though, if you are in relationship with both God and them. Talking, asking, praying, listening, going where God is leading and where you are invited.

In case you hadn't heard, there is an on-going debate about short-term ministry trips. Are they worth the cost? Would it be better to just send the money? Are we doing these trips because they make us feel better or because they're truly helpful? These are excellent questions that must be asked and answered. David Livermore's *Serving with Eyes Wide Open* gives a great overview of the challenges and possible solutions. *Helping Without Hurting in Short-Term Missions* from the Chalmers Center is another fantastic resource. Both point out that short-term trips can, and often do, cause more harm than good. *But that doesn't mean we should stop doing them altogether. It means we should stop doing them poorly.*

I'll echo what both of those books declare: the trip shouldn't be the end goal. It should be part of a bigger strategy and plan, namely an on-going relationship with a global partner. Consequently, our visits should be initiated by the leaders in the host country and should play a part in the partnership strategy. Our trips should be driven by the same principle and the best practices discussed in chapter seven, that drive our partnerships. Even though they are short-term, they should be done with long-term impact in mind. They should center on developing leaders and building capacity rather than meeting needs and inadvertently creating dependency. Team participants should do *with* the people in the host community rather than doing *for* them. Our trips should be focused on going deep in a few places rather than scattering ourselves all over lots of places. *Short-term trips shouldn't be done away with; they should be done better.* When they're done well, they provide an irreplaceable opportunity to build the kinds of relationships that lead to transformation.

Go where you are invited. Go on the trip or at least to the information meeting. Go across the ocean or at least across the street. Go to a new culture or at least go meet the new neighbor. Don't forget: Jesus came to start a movement, not build a monument. So get moving. Start going. Step toward that opportunity that God has put in front of you. Take a step. Make a move. Go!

Everyone Can Walk This Way

Pray specifically. Give wisely. Go where you are invited. These three steps provide an opportunity for everyone to get in the game. No one needs to stay on the bench. There's a part for each person – young, old, rich, poor, singles, couples and families – to play in the global story God is writing. No one has to do everything. Everyone can do something. Together we can be part of something grand and global.

And when we focus our praying, giving and going toward the same people and places, the impact can be significant. Teams can visit the school that was built with the funds that were raised. Sponsors can help more students attend that very school, while prayer

emboldens the national leaders to keep up the good but hard work. A future funding drive could make it possible to pipe clean water to that same school, giving the students and their families easy access to safe water. A ministry team may be able to join in the manual labor as trenches are dug and pipes are laid. All the while, the local leaders in the community, the ones on the Leadership Council forging the way, earn much-deserved respect for leading the community in this direction. Churches and believers are unified and strengthened as they love and serve their community. The people of God, both locally and globally, are seen as the ones who are making things better in this community. Spiritual conversations result, growing the church in size and strength. It's a beautiful thing. That's where this path leads. And it starts when we pray, give and go.

"We make the road by walking."

My favorite African proverb is, "We make the road by walking." I love the imagery. You can picture the well-worn dirt path curving through a field – like the one in Kenya, pictured on the previous page.

Other paths aren't in wide, open spaces, but instead cut through the thick bush and overgrowth. Have you ever thought about how the path became well worn? It wasn't always that way. In fact, at one point there was no path at all. At some point, someone needed to blaze a trail from here to there. Hacking a way through the bush that very first time was difficult and painful. The next several trips were too. But over time, especially as more and more people moved down the path, the trail became clear, well defined, easier to navigate. It will probably never be perfectly straight or totally level, but it doesn't have to be. It just has to get us from here to there. And it does that quite well.

Global partnerships are like that path. We don't have a clear, smooth highway to move down. We're setting out on a walk, a long walk. We have a general idea of where God is going, but we will still have to make the path one step at a time. We'll do well to remember that we're walking down the paths of proclamation, compassion and justice, giving a glimpse of the restoration that God will one day unfold.

The best thing we can do is walk the path together, shoulder-to-shoulder and heart-to-heart with God's people across the globe. The first steps we can take along the path are praying specifically, giving wisely, and going where we are invited. It's uncharted and exciting, but we're not going alone. God has prepared the way for us and is surely in this place. He's inviting us to walk with Him down the path of transformation. What are we waiting for? Let's walk this way!

START WALKING
Notes and Next Steps

Walk This Way: What Now?
- Pray specifically.
- Give wisely.
- Go where you are invited.

Next Steps
- Begin a life-changing connection with a child and their community by **sponsoring a student** through 410 Bridge (www.410Bridge.org) or Canopy Life Academy (www.CanopyLife.org).
- Prepare your teams for effective and healthy short-term ministry trips with Fikkert and Corbett's *Help Without Hurting in Short-Term Missions.*
- Join the journey at **www.WalkThisWay.world**.

RESOURCES AND REFERENCES

Chapter 1

Matthew 4:19, 8:22, 9:9, 10:38, 16:24, 19:21, 19:28; Mark 1:17, 2:14, 8:34, 10:21; Luke 5:27, 9:23, 9:59, 14:27, 18:22; John 1:43, 8:12, 10:27, 12:26, 13:36, 21:19 and 21:22.

Chapter 2

- Barrett, D., & Johnson, T. (2001). *World Christian Trends AD 30 - AD 2200: Interpreting the Annual Christian Megacensus.* Pasadena, CA: William Carey Library.
- The Future of World Religions: Population Growth Projections, 2010-2050 http://www.pewforum.org/2015/04/02/religious-projections-2010-2050 (accessed April 2015).
- Wright, C. (January 2007). "An Upside-Down World." *Christianity Today.*

Chapter 3

- Livermore, D. (accessed April 2013). "Ten Things I Hate About American Missions Projects." http://davidlivermore.com/wp content/uploads/2011/03/10_things_hate_m_proj.pdf.
- Saint, S. (2009). *Missions Dilemma.* Dunnellon, FL: I-TEC Press.
- Elmer, D. (2006). *Cross-Cultural Servanthood.* Downers Grove, IL: InterVarsity Press.

Chapter 4

- Bestall, C. (2001). *Killers Don't Cry* and *Killers Come Home.* British Broadcasting Corporation.
- Yancey, P. (2010) *What Good is God?* New York: FaithWords.

Chapter 5
- Dooling, R. (1995). *White Man's Grave.* London: Picador.
- Muriu, O. "Partnership: The Body of Christ." (*Partners Worldwide.* Internet. Available from http://www.youtube.com/watch?v=FS7_Bf0Idw0).

Chapter 6
- Fikkert, B., & Corbett, S. (2009). *When Helping Hurts.* Chicago: Moody.
- Stearns, R. (2010). *The Hole in Our Gospel.* Nashville: Thomas Nelson.

Chapter 7
- Elmer, D. (2006). *Cross-Cultural Servanthood.* Downers Grove, IL: InterVarsity Press.
- Fikkert, B., & Corbett, S. (2009). *When Helping Hurts.* Chicago: Moody.
- Lupton, R. (2011). *Toxic Charity.* Harper Collins.
- Rickett, D. (2008). *Building Strategic Relationships.* Minneapolis: Stem Press.
- Rickett, D. (2015). *Making Your Partnerships Work.* Roswell, GA: Daniel Rickett.

Chapter 8
Rickett, D. (2015). *Making Your Partnerships Work.* Roswell, GA: Daniel Rickett.

Chapter 9
- Baterson, M. (2011). *The Circle Maker.* Grand Rapids: Zondervan.
- Mandryk, J. (2010). *Operation World.* Downer's Grove: IVP Books.
- Martin, J. (2008). *Giving Wisely?* Sister, OR.: Last Chapter Publishing.

- Wydick, B. (June 2013). "Want to Change the World? Sponsor a Child," *Christianity Today.* Available at http://www.christianitytoday.com/ct/2013/june/want-to-change-world-sponsor-child.html
- Livermore, D. (2013). *Serving with Eyes Wide Open: Doing Short-Term Missions with Cultural Intelligence.* Grand Rapids: Baker Books.
- Corbett, S., & Fikker, B. (2014). *Help Without Hurting in Short-Term Missions.* Chicago: Moody.

ABOUT THE AUTHOR

Born in Zimbabwe, and the great-grandson of Irish immigrants, Paul's upbringing and cross-cultural exposure have given him a unique perspective on international engagement. For more than a decade, Paul has led the Global Outreach initiatives of Parker Hill Church, a thriving multi-site church in Northeast Pennsylvania. He has had the opportunity to train church leaders in large and small group settings both in the states and abroad in countries like Germany, Kenya, and Haiti.

Paul's passion is mobilizing people to engage in what God is doing around the world. This often means moving from a traditional missionary approach to an innovative engagement in global partnerships. Under Paul's leadership, and through collaboration with the 410 Bridge, Parker Hill has formed healthy and sustainable alliances in Kenya and Haiti. In both places, American believers are coming alongside national leaders in an effort to move toward Christ-centered, community-initiated development.

Paul earned a bachelor's degree from Summit University, and went on to earn degrees in master of ministry and doctor of ministry programs. Paul is married to Aimee, his high school sweetheart, and has four children: Mattie, Jackson, Andie and Ella. They spend their days traveling, laughing with friends, and organizing family talent shows.

Made in the USA
Middletown, DE
19 March 2019